UNCOMMON

Johnny Francis Wolf

.

Pushcart nominated
author of

MEN UNLIKE OTHERS

A Wild Ink Publishing Original
Wild Ink Publishing
wild-ink-publishing.com

ISBN: (Hardcover) 978-1-958531-71-6
ISBN: (Paperback) 978-1-958531-72-3

When I met Johnny online, back in 2009, I had no idea what a willful and wonderful detour life would soon take.

I went through a divorce not too long after, jumped in an RV with my cats, a parrot named Peanut, my youngest son, and off we went to see the world. We made it to New Mexico where Johnny came to visit that Christmas. Some time later, looking for a place to settle down for a short while, I considered California, not far from Johnny. A short while became three years with, yes, your author as my next door neighbor.

At this point one was never without the other. Three years turned to six, with the last few as housemates in New Mexico.

When we shared our creations, one on one (words, designs, and art), the inspiration seemed to flow back and forth. Wonderful verses came tumbling out of him in the middle of his, then, script writing. From that seed grew his poetry with me as cheerleader... writing poems myself, as well.

I found the more I could get him to write, the more I also wrote.

Funny, us odd people, what we discover about ourselves living with others likewise odd. He will always be a member of my family, brother from another mother, as it were.

Keep on writing, my friend.

Rhonda Lynne Wingo
Poet, Writer, Artist, avid Gardner, Photographer
Forever Friend and Fan
Wolfhaven20@hotmail.com

As the Lynne Spins, Facebook (poetry)
Wolf-n-Drake Studios, Facebook (art)
Wolf-n-Drake Photography, Facebook (images)

Dedication

The formative years can be daunting when one is odd.

And I was markedly so all throughout grade school. Even my musings were skewed.. the silent rantings of someone whose inner editor was off on a deserted island scribing letters in the sand, sending postcards to absolutely no one, and praying for skywriters to render his thoughts into puffy cloud font.

My observations on life and god and loving one's fellow man were scrupulously formed by my sixth year.

They were:

I will excel as both altar boy and saint (maybe martyr) dutifully following the exacting Catholic credo as ascribed by my mother.

I will live up to my three older brothers' reputation for wielding high IQs.

I will be married, in due course, to a woman who looked remarkably like my First Grade teacher, Mrs. Lark. We will reside in Arkansas, making a living plowing fields on our undoubtedly many acres.

(Not sure where the latter aspiration came from, but watching MODERN FARMER Saturday mornings before the cartoons may have played a role.)

Oh.. and my fondness for naked GI Joes (as opposed to my school yard pals' partiality for stripped Barbie dolls) would be a fleeting and soonly fading fancy. Surely.

By Sixth Grade, I was full-on weird.

And like many queerly fashioned and singular 12-year-olds, I endeavored to compete in every Science Fair my school sponsored (Spring and Fall).

I did so to prove how normal I was, participating in such enjoyable, rollicking wisdom fests. The diametric obverse is actually what one broadcasts to the free world, competing in such disesteemed and wholly frowned upon.. nerd clambakes.

My Spring entry, that year, was dissecting a Perch.

Today's animal-lover Johnny was less squeamish about slicing open dead fish back then. In fact, it was fishing, in general, that afforded me and my father our only connection. Of course, I would ALWAYS toss them back in the lake (lovely Summers in Pennsylvania) and ALWAYS with a baits-worth of worm or bread in their mouths. Payment for their inconvenience.

My poster board was covered with scotch-taped tear sheets and magic-markered smears regaling my non-existent audience with biological facts and anatomical trivia, extolling the wondrous nature of all things Perch.

I won a special Runner-Up ribbon, that May.

The Seventh and Eighth Graders were rapt with how I pronounced "Perch". My lip contortions when intoning the "r" were apparently too knotted to ignore (all fifty times the word was uttered during my memorized presentation).

This speech aberration inspired Beavis and Butt-Head snickering throughout most of my unwaveringly positive and fixedly delivered pitch on fish. Their laughter propelled me forward.. proud and ashamed and unflinching, somehow.

I dedicate my book to him.

Me at 12 years old.

Introduction

I can't recall her exact words. It was the first review conferred upon my new Daily Poem Fan Page. The reviewer and I were, yet, official Facebook friends.

"I would like to sit beneath a tree.. alone in a grove, sipping a cool drink. I crack the book's spine, flip through its pages. My head finds a soft place, leaning against the tree's yielding bark.. the blanket beneath me, plaid and fuzzy. I spend my afternoon reading Johnny's verse.."

or something quite similar. A poet as well, it would surprise no one familiar with her style were the exact words even more balmy than those my memory managed to summon up.

Ayo Gutierrez thusly first reached out.

Seems most of the reviews on my Page have fallen victim to Facebook's many subsequent schematic revisions (with Ayo's appraisal, sadly, one of the missing). But the impression it made was lasting. It's never too far from my heart when I raise a quill or tap on a keyboard.

—

And write, I did, daily and more. A dribble, a deluge, depending the day.

The online sharing was everything, the comments from friends were kinder than I deserved, the encouragement enlivening.

I would not be a writer today had I not braved the internet criticism (received plenty) and risked the potential online plagiarism (though I've always held such social media word thieves could find better bards to steal from).. had I not sought out an audience to tender my tales.

I am forever indebted to the mentors I met, the friendships I forged, the learning-by-reading the brilliant words they, too, shared on Facebook.

—

Mine are bald and artless yarns with thorny roots and frizzy leaves. Some feel unfinished. All remain unpolished.

I'm nervous revisiting this simpler time, rereading the runes of someone more dewy-eyed.. inking, as I did then, with impulsive and unguarded ease.

Uncommon, seems.

Left to my own devices, I might hide these prequel iterations.

The resulting primordial ooze now sits before you.. a gathering of raw, awkward phrases and sing-songy rhymes that dare the reader to look past the grammar (or lack thereof) and find the bold, unripened core, the pits, the pith..

the skin unpeeled.

—

Now Ayo, my first mentor.. an esteemed author, teacher, and acclaimed publisher in her own right.. has her book.

"Can I find you a tree, offer a cool drink, dear friend? I may have a blanket to lend.."

Angels

Christmas

Food

Hieroglyphics

Me & Hue

Naughty

Realm

Similitude

Angels

Above

Fleshy sprites of hallowed heft,
    feathered wings with sturdy weft.

Gaze upon the clouds on high,
    cherubs chubby ponder sky.

Windswept locks, zephyr's whirl,
    upward eyes neath tress's curl.

Ample angels, prayerful staring,
    sainted seraphs, holy pairing.

Choir raising, praising Lord,
    that alone its own reward.

Makes me wonder why so round..
    Yon heaven's gate, is pizza found?

afire

(angel lit)

Was certain I would meet her,

      as moth in black
         I know of light.

The when was never sweeter

      with nary lack
         of appetite.

: :

To flame I'm drawn without a doubt,

      my feathers burnt,
         wings too charred.

Teary-eyed and mine in drought,

      her grace unlearnt
         as skin unscarred.

: :

Sizzled, screaming.. slipping life,

      drank her sorrow,
         sipping dry.

Her love I licked off crimson knife,

      soul I borrowed,
         rest will buy.

Pray to god to pardon me,

nigh contrite,
        on knee I fall.

I lie... my will, I harden thee,

as yearn to bite,
        ignite them all.

bereft of title, picture

(angel changed)

entered screaming, flailing arms
led by lips and words

quill as sword unsheathed her charms
anger quelled in thirds

::

seeming waltz she danced upon
ajar, the raptured shell

lost her footing, eyes of fawn
unfurled the Prince of Hell

::

reached akimbo, limbered grasp
taunting tail with burn

perfect union, imp and asp
and dust that lives in urn

Box of Angels
(Spring 2013)

Spied a solid gray Pit Bull darting between cars. Was a few blocks from where I live. Beautiful pup. Maybe 9 months old, 40 pounds-ish.. careening in and out of traffic.

No leash, collar or tags. I parked, fixed a loose rope around his neck (completely unnecessary as he followed me everywhere), and endeavored to find his owner. I knocked on several nearby doors.. ringing bells, hollering up at open windows.

My Los Angeles neighborhood has a gated community feel to it, with me, no doubt, pegged as some sweaty, recently escaped prison inmate (in truth, returning weary from the gym).

No one answered their door.

Took him home. I have no room in my tiny pool house digs, and two wary cats not terribly welcoming of strays.

:::

Went online, found a shelter open late, hour and a half away. Drove there with this sweet pie of a puppy licking my ears and nose and neck, trying with all his might to jump in my lap.

Not an easy drive, but a wonderful one. And wholly sad.. envisioning the return trip, alone.

Lady at the shelter.. sooooo very nice. She was convinced he'd have a microchip (was too well-groomed, too well-fed not to).. but wouldn't be able to check 'til morning.

She was in love with him immediately, same as I. Thought.. my gosh, if he doesn't have a chip, I kinda hope she adopts him.

They'd be a good match.

I'm not worried about him. He's handsome, strong and loving. He *WILL* find a home.. no question.

: :

Walking to my car, I met some folks carrying an old, cardboard box full of three straggly, dirty white mutts. Likely dreamed up by Dr. Seuss, later deigned too scrawny even by his publishers.. each appeared littler, sweeter, more drawn than the next..

angels, really.

Family's house is nestled in a cul-de-sac near a sanitation site. Folks dump their dogs just feet from their yard.. I guess when they no longer want them. (How is that possible?) The family has already adopted many such pups. Couldn't handle any more.

These beaten-down babies in a cardboard box broke my heart. I pray they find homes.

: :

Please..
you pray too.

compact

renowned for her beauty, known for her clothes
    a model and maybe a ghost

covers for Vogue, a signature pose
    could float down the runway, almost

: :

smoothing foundation, glossing her lips
    painful to see her own face

never as whole, would view them in chips
    cracked was the mirror she'd grace

: :

several sets of cheekbones to blush
    the real estate cut into parts

make-up applied with liner and brush
    myriad slices and charts

: :

twenty-five eyes to shadow with blue
    with too many lashes to curl

plenty of pieces to color and hue
    was never the only one girl

: :

left humble behind when front of the lens
    camera who loved her like verse

then make-up removed, done with her cleanse
    shards that she slipped in her purse

: :

(the story was told to me by a good friend in my youth while dealing with my own body-dysmorphic issues.. I remember the model in question as Jean Shrimpton, or perhaps it was Suzy Parker...

when doing her own make-up, she'd use a compact with a cracked mirror.. allowing her to see countless views of one square inch at a time...

if more than that, viewed as a whole, was too ugly for her to witness)

dress

(airing out on fire escape)

and if I thought the color odd
            scarlet with a ginger tinge

it hung there like an Act of God
                  crowd below would come unhinged

grin and stare and echo awe
            at yards and yards of crinoline

us looking up with slackened jaw
                  as wondered who the mannequin

: :

'Rescue me!' I thought I heard..
        'Save me from the high school prom!'

while fit and flare attracted birds
                  a silk and satin cluster bomb

were polka dotted droppings soon
            where left alone to ape a flag

rain and stars and sun and moon
                  still envied by the boys in drag

: :

remaining for the better part
       of March through almost end of May

made me laugh.. this work of art
          for up I'd gaze but every day

and lastly when it disappeared
       unsure it didn't fly on gust

gone was gown and felt quite weird
        to miss our bit of angel dust

fragments

(of a roller disco)

wasn't really like that, MUCH
a dream, you know.. felt more like SUCH

if something vaguely physical, less than flimsy
hardly fuzzy, fewer oddly-
umbrous THINGS

were happenchance-ly flapping WINGS...

and yet quite REAL, tho nearly HID
I went with it on even KEEL, until I didn't (mostly DID)
as strapped them up with laces TEAL
polished leather, sparkly
WHEELS..

said nothing really give me PAUSE as knew
he was angelic-ISH

showed me things in lightened GAUZE, could feel
his dark, adorning WISH...

we skirted past some splurgy MIST and darted
through a billowed BRUME
when comets flamed a path through THIS, their very center
corpus ROOM..

celestial orbs and painted planets...
lumened stars from
disco BALL

just waiting for the perfect time to skate around a rink

is ALL

glisten

light would bend to hide all trace
her brightness all but lit the space

candles seemed to flicker, flare
choked as if by lack of air

entered rooms with sparks and slips
rays would drip from burning lips

wet with blaze and glazed with gleam
when spilling fire, burning dreams

songs she whispered, window's glare
dawn she stole as sun not there

Jumpers

(parachuting into war)

Like jellyfish with good intent,
for readied landing, knees at bent.

    FLOATING FREELY, fear inert —
    dropping, ditching — spitting dirt.

How to navigate the two:
First you're FLYING, then you FLEW.

    Breathing only Angel air
    as soaring over Demon lair.

If allowed, my verse conceit,
above the FIELDS of burning wheat —

    swimming, sailing — would we know
    world engulfed in FLAMES below.

Kaepernick's Prayer

explain again, I soon forget
        how taking knee dishonors vet..

how bowing head, if arm in arm
        defiles flag, elicits harm...

when genuflecting near to earth
        a heart's more nigh to nation's birth

is closer to the waves of grain
        to soldiers dying not in vain

humbles one before their God
        with knee in dirt as pressing sod

banded with the others who
        are forced to cringe and cower new

'til Black Lives Matter justice done
        we stand together, kneel as one

is not a war 'tween BLACK and BLUE
        when raise him up, I raise up you

matinee

(maple leaf or butterfly)

movie-making thicket far
    billing battle, who the star

butterflies seem mostly rise
    leaves will fall as Summer dies

which is which and who is who
    one was dancing, other flew

spewing lines akin to prose
    one goes fast as other slows

cinematic focused scope
    understanding story, nope

critics pan the simple plot
    good beginning, middle not

shiftings drift upon a breeze
    fly-er, flee-er switch with ease

God as fickle film auteur
    happy ending, still unsure

Night

(is split)

Bluest blue
with royal hue,
evening dew

    in midnight's cauldron, sacred brew.

Dreaming of
a mourning dove,
flames in love

    glare and glisten, gleam above.

Evil's truth
is glowing proof,
lasting youth

    drips from trees like sweet vermouth.

Poison bird
in tainted word,
death interred

    is singing dirges, lyrics slurred.

Hope of dawn
when angels warn,
heaven's scorn

    'til light and life again reborn.

Origin

(Moirai)

polychromic, freckled, veined
BIBLE swears it's all explained

springs from fountain, spitting LIFE
dappled, marbled, speckled rife

like my SECRETS more obscure
enigmatic, cryptic, pure

trust the angels know my FATE
witless me will blithely wait

CONSTELLATIONS open wide
divination mystified

prefer my God remote and RARE
as gaze at stars..   am lost in prayer

School

FLAXEN WAVES framed her face,
were swept and tamed with borrowed comb.
A camel coat like SWADDLE
draped, robed her
shoulders, regal stole.

Spotlight lighting just her chair,
royal klieg that flooded
there.

Chrysalis with blameless face,
pink and peach and
EGGSHELL
bone.

Birthed and bare and still untold —

And though NO COLORS bled from picture —
knew that hers
were SHADES of GOLD.

::

The rest of them were
BLACK and WHITE.
Students,
mostly gray.

Some, too close,
RECEIVED HER LIGHT —
Pearls were in their gaze, there even
as they LOOKED AWAY. Nacre loosed from shiny eyes.

And I was there and in that class,
a DIFFERENT SCHOOL from distant year
in disparate room —

but SAME the photo, likewise
RAPT as wrapped
in glim,
enfolded womb.

: :

Fear — excited, OVERWHELMED —

Trying not to sweat.
Trying hard to color wet.
Trying gilded shades on lips.
Trying pearls from eyes and hips.

NONE of us stood out
like she —

But deep inside
we had
her
light.

I WILLED MYSELF
to have
her
light.

Reason, still, all stars and I
are burnished golden, BLAZING BRIGHT.

(Marilyn Monroe, attending class at the Actors Studio,
New York City, 1955)

shed

less to do for scapulae
        if fewer tufts upon

ailerons seem quiver free
        their feathers folded, drawn

age of flutter, soaring 'bove
        for aeons, focused high

choosing mud, this wingless dove
        has no more need to fly

now I love in human form
        falling, my ballet

naked flesh, the sun too warm
        with plumage melting 'way

starving artist

when did it happen like this
that all of these things

keeping me safe, secure in a
world with roof
and car

a bed of my own
food to eat, now all out of reach

why did I shun the corporate world
and think I could live

on ink and paint

: :

nothing left for wife nor lover
children, cats and dogs

nor me

money not free, not easy to pry from
hands who hold it dear

: :

pay not for pictures nor poet's voice
but save it for that

which someone else whispers

(screams) in your ear

things that you need much more than mine

more than words or colors in songs
that rhyme with heart

than pay for
art

: :

things you swear allow you
your stuff, your joy
enough

like cars that drive and park themselves
and Amazon boxes with
magic within

devices that play the songs we've sung

the singers who need a meal

: :

and still I serve you blues that drip

from sky and easel, palette
and brush

books from bards and ballads unsung

bleats from horn as bleed from eye, viscous clear
in hat upturned to welcome your coin

begging for crumbs

to eat

Those that Sit and Judge

Life's too short to waste concerned

with other people's rules.

Let them be their love unlearned

in irreligious schools.

undulating

(fine art)

scale the heights
        and clamber peaks

air is light
        so fill your cheeks

                : :

fill hers too
        as aim to please

loving view
        ascend with ease

                : :

hike the trail
        that leads to warm

probing vale
        where men belong

                : :

rooted cleft
        and tight the crack

curves with heft
        neath nether back

                : :

tour the valleys
        ski her slopes

searching alleys
        tie with ropes

: :

buried deep
        when apex high

soon too steep
        the ending nigh

: :

spire lording
        over crest

summit reached
        and need to rest

: :

journey blind
        with guided touch

thank her kindly
        Climb here much?

UNTIMELY

"I'll meet you here at 10..."

His words fell flat.

In the thickening pause, her eyes
willed themselves to smile.

"I might be late," she teased with a
pirated grin.

"I'm....." she started, stumbling.
"I've been known to be late, sometimes."

He knew.

::

Deaf to the irony swimming around like sperms
about an egg.. her own reveal of
cycles late...

she vowed tonight would tell him firm.

He'd be a Father almost 7
months, few days
from now.

Time enough for May
and flowers.

::

Her monthly friend was never tardy...
girl who's always late
for dinner

..always
last to know.

He knew that, too.

::

She arrived in the Square ten minutes early.

Applied the last of her,

*"Please ask me to marry you,
I can't raise a child alone,"* makeup...

Straightened her shortest skirt,
already too tight at
the waist.

::

He never showed for dinner,
never showed for
ever.

Winter came to Prague
that night

.....too many months 'til Spring.

within

strange how tears can spark a fire
when quench the flames, they should

odd when wet can quell desire
eyes are blind to good

: :

I follow what my brain reveals
as listen with my heart

deaf to what my body feels
awaken with a start

: :

bolt, I rise, now facing God
His wrath is plainly spoke

naked both, He drives his rod
from where it pierces..   smoke

: :

thereupon a spark ignites
my cries are muted mews

flickers glow like thousand lights
ablaze, I stand accused

: :

"did you think I'd let you live
and write the words you wrote..

spewing truth with love you give..."
'twas then He slashed my throat

: :

afloat above the floor, it seemed
forever would I burn

woke, it was a dream I dreamed
and every night return

Christmas

3d

red and ***green*** as black and white
glasses twist their line of sight

       tricking vantage, depth of view
  as angle, pitch and distance skew

red and ***green*** as Christmas Eve
then and now I interweave

       stretching aspect shortens time
  of youth and aging, passing prime

red and ***green*** as stop and go
traffic lights preserving flow

       space and season, SUV
  like colors bending what we see

http://www.life.com/arts-entertainment/3-d-movies-revisiting-a-classic-life-photo-of-a-rapt-film-audience/

bed

fuzzy flannel, furry fleece

       feathered pillows.. thank you, geese

sueded trim on wooly throw

       solid pine, the berth below

      : :

ombre plaid is crimson hued

       neath the blanket, mostly nude

counting sheep for needed rest

       more than bed, a quilted nest

      : :

snowy drifts block morning view

       warmly spooning, me and you

help.. please rescue, shovel, save

       not till April.. we'll be brave

Blue Star

I'm new in this town, just me and my cats,
    a gift shoppe nearby with tchotchke and hats.

My favorite new neighbor, her birthday today,
    I bought her a star, all blue glass inlay.

Hung from a chain of brass-finished pewter,
    hoping she'd like it, I thought it might suit her.

If lumens are needed and light that you lack..
    a tiffany door hiding candle in back.

Out from the star glowed azure and sky
    from prisms and points, on everyone nigh.

We liked it so much I had to buy two,
    went back there anon as stood in their queue.

"You still have in stock the votive light star
    that shines like a sapphire jewel from afar?"

"Indeed!" they exclaimed. I bought it forsooth
    and hung it that night, 'tis God's honest truth.

And there from our ceilings, both neighbor's and mine,
　　our stars shining bright over Cuervos with lime.

Sterling and I, a lull in our chat,
　　looked upward and stared.. sipped, savored and sat.

Home to her own, leaving mousers and me,
　　Los Angeles life, an Actor I'll be.

That's what the star, maybe, symbolized most,
　　those Walk of Fame maps and Hollywood ghosts.

I light it when worried I'm oafish and old,
　　as brings me back home to the snow and the cold.

I'm missing New York, the starlight reveals,
　　its concrete and glass, its girders and steel.

But here amongst palm trees, flip flops and sun,
　　I'm wishing on new stars and seeking new fun.

New friends I have met, not many but few..
　　no Acting successes, but still I'm not through.

My finances grim, Recession began
　　as late with the rent, all very unplanned.

A milestone birthday, a buddy named Doug
　　(seems always more birthdays.. just sayin', I shrug).

But this was a doozy, not one to dismiss,
    no mere Hallmark card, manly hug or air kiss.

Thinking of theories I thought I could try,
    without too much money 'twas little could buy.

A gift's gotta hurt a trifle, I knew,
    then into my heart a tiny bird flew.

"Give him the star you cherish each night..."
    That's crazy, I thought. It doesn't seem right.

But felt in a flash that's what I must do,
    as clutching my star found polish and glue.

Chain a bit fragile but sturdy enough,
    was kinda like me, all gritty and tough.

I polished the metal and mended the links.
    "Looks almost like new!" untangling chinks.

Buffed up the glass, had been a few years,
    all inside and out as smoothed out the smears.

Wiped off the soot from the candlelight shimmer,
    and burnished the beryl, increasing its glimmer.

I used it a lot, was worse for the wear,
    as life makes us weary. I sat in my chair.

It cleaned up quite good and that we share too,
    cerulean glass, my irises blue.

For just one more night, it lit up my room,
    fell soundly asleep as morning came soon.

Woke with a start, a cat in my lap,
    rushing around, nearly noon.. *holy crap.*

Kitties meowing for food, hale and hearty,
    as served them their mush. I'll be late for the party.

Grabbed for the star, some tissues and wrappings,
    swathed it in Christmas and Birthdays and scrapings.

Tied up the votives, as wished I had more,
    with pieces of ribbon.. as knocking on door.

"Frankenstein gift for you, my good friend."
    The feeling of missing my starlight will end.

A piece of my soul delivered that day
    with whimsical, wondrous wishes, I pray.

The Gift of the Magi, an O. Henry tale..
    if comes from the heart still liable to fail.

An ultimate something you really don't need,
    this cheap piece of metal and glass, I concede.

Like beauty that ripens with wisdom and wine,
    a friendship fermenting and moldy with time.

Are hard fought our battles, 'tween two and alone.
    Please, give my blue star a suitable home.

Addendum:

Christmas following his noteworthy birthday fête, the actor,
Doug Jones, left a red tiffany star upon my doorstep.

If it were possible, was even lovelier
than my own blue.

From the Land of Misfit Toys

A friend and her husband have health issues, limited funds...
and grandchildren they adore.

The *other* in-laws are able to shower the kids with flashy and
fabulous gifts.. high-tech, TikTok trending, viral, expensive
everything.. presented with flourish and flare and lots of
fanfare. And the kids just eat it up.

My friends cannot do this.

:::

Instead, Grandpa goes down to the Thrift Shop each month to
see what's 'new', poring through the children's books and used
toy bins.. searching for a treasure. And sometimes he finds
one.

At the end of his day, Santa's helper brings home his trove of
plum and prized and precious pearls.. all bought for 4 dollars
and 58 cents. With maybe a can of Lysol.

And that's when Grandma and Grandpa get busy.

:::

Patches to the dolly's dresses, washed and pressed, their faces
scrubbed. Safe enamel paint applied to Tonka trucks with
scratches, to Matchbox cars in need of a makeover, to the
dollhouse windows and flower boxes.. to the teeny-tiny fruits
in the eensy-weensy fruit bowl on the itsy-bitsy kitchen table.

Taping pages torn.. neatened, trimmed, corners un-folded.
Covers, bindings set and straightened. Pencil marks erased.

Trains repaired and rubbed and rubbed until they shine like new. Engine wheels all well-aligned. Train tracks glued and welded. Little, plastic buildings fixed with toothpicks, paste and paint. Mini people's hair touched-up and coiffed with magic markers. Small, fuzzy fir trees fussed with, sparkly snow now laid atop.

Weebles worked 'til wobble wightly. Legos grouped by size and color as placed in fancy stogie boxes.

Bicycles wiped and oiled.. waxed. Flat tires patched and filled. Horns tuned to just the right honk. Bells adjusted 'til tingles sound jingly. Baseball cards clothes-pinned to wheel spokes for clickety-clack *vroooooooms!*

Woolite-laundered teddy bears have their bellies stuffed and fluffed with old and doughy pillow down. Unruly bunny rabbit ears are surgically set with Singer machine stitch witchery.

Puppy dog tails made waggable again.. tacked in tight as toes attached. Buttons sewn where eyes were missing. Balding kitties given whiskers.

: :

All wrapped up with something special from the secret stash of Grandma's favorite, most delicately un-wrapped and un-taped, re-gifted and re-used.. legendary wrapping paper supply.

Never you mind what Holiday it's for.. if it's pretty, has no untended-to rips or straggly corners and frizzled edges.. then all it needs is some festive ribbon trickery (at least 3 different strands of 3 divergent colors, all cut and curled with scissors) and a glorious contrasting bow (with a loop of extra tape beneath, to help the tired glue)...

..and you got yourself a Merry Christmas, Happy Bar Mitzvah, and/or Bestest Birthday *EVER!!*

And while a brand new Barbie, Baby Shark, Apple i-Whatever
gets the firstest, biggest, loudest SHOUTS..

a Grandma, Grandpa gifting of

invention, care, attention, love...

..is opened as if made of gold

with oohs and aahs a hundredfold

(a truly special thing behold)...

for ancient gifts cannot grow old.

FROZEN

(empathetic friends)

Frigid and stiff if polar like PEA,
    the further you ROLL — and probably key.

Firming our fears all frosty with STARCH
    CRISPENS our step as forwards our march.

WIGGLE your toes — ignoring the fact
    if ever they're numb, it's part of an ACT.

Snow from the NORTH, wind from the WEST —
    PEAS IN A POD can help with the rest.

Warm is okay, but COOL even better.
    NERVOUS is fine — can borrow my sweater.

gravitas

it's not the big and showy things
first 3 entries — one's obit

       but maybe more the words unwrit
       between the lines — that softly

       cite how loved they were
       — by kids and dogs

smiles and winks on Friday nights
watching *Frozen* — yet again

holding tiny hands
with her who
hardly

breathes unless
— to sing

       popcorn fingers licked
       by pup who
       hardly

       laps unless —
       to love

ILLUME

Candle's flame is burning wax,
DRIPPING HONEY, molten tracks.

Window cracked with breeze between,
shadows dance like HALLOWEEN.

FUELED by wick as FED by air,
illuminating everywhere..

Tiny KITCHEN, Ballroom GRANDE,
recipe or music stand.

Shining bright for all it's worth
when favors NO ONE lighting Earth.

Never kindles any less..
STATELY SPREAD or watercress.

leaving

this year I think
I'm going
home

a place I thought did not
exist but Christmas
Eve and when

my Mom put bandaids
on my knees
(a lot)

and finally the buzz that shook
her being, manic
movements
dulled

eyes that matched her smile
again would leave
her lips

upon my cheek with 'russet rose' by Maybelline

: :

soon, I can afford a car
and head back

East

to where..

I hardly know

                    : :

but close to home
or close
enuf

at least it will be
far from
here

and nearer to
beneath the green
and towards the blue is

where my Mom now calls her

home

nightlight

painted plaster, beryl blue

    as lit by candle's fuzzy view

nigh to sky than wall of paste

    is more like moon than flame encased

candelabra's barefaced glow

    on naked ceiling, room below

outdoor feeling, indoor air

    when twilight kindles evening's lair

lying lantern after dark

    our night rebuffed by fire's spark

golden faces freshly brushed

    will further fable, blackness crushed

http://www.youtube.com/watch?v=4KiFSKLTj0U

ODE to SNOWY JOEY

Bloody balls in silhouette,
his frigid carcass bleeding yet.
Finished job, removed the threat,
when LOPPING HEAD with bayonet.

    Story is as old as time,
    Zombie Snowman, CRIMSON CRIME.
    Cold and mute, this grisly mime,
    for eating brains and reindeer slime.

Began like any other day,
a CHRISTMAS EVE with human prey.
Blizzard brought him on his sleigh,
all guts and glory, death, decay.

    His snowy globes were stacked in three,
    was sizing up my family, me.
    Ate my son with YULETIDE GLEE..
    drank my daughter's blood, like tea.

I punched his crooked carrot nose,
and KICKED the COAL he used for toes.
Started shooting when I froze
as watched him slowly decompose.

    But knew, a fan of WALKING DEAD,
    I must remove his snowball head.
    When knifed the neck it spurted red,
    stabbed his brains, the sanguine spread.

Rolling off, it hit the ground,
I TOOK a BREATH and looked around.
With no more family, not a sound,
our "Silent Night" in scarlet drowned.

Here we are as we began,
my tale of FROSTED BOOGEYMAN.
Tearing up, I had no plan
as turned to flee.. yes, cried and ran.

The Holidays are full of dangers,
Zombies hid in Christmas Mangers.
Next time call on Texas Rangers,
never welcome FROZEN STRANGERS.

That is it, no more to tell,
are NO MORE JINGLES in my bell,
no more singing "First Noel".
Snowy Joey melts in Hell.

PRODIGAL

BORNE of rapture, earthly bound,
as sirens sang without a sound.

Christened CHASTE in rivers pure,
was cold the current, swift the cure.

: :

'Til fell from GRACE at ransom's cost
when longing, leaping.   Soul was lost.

Lord, FORGIVE your wayward Son
with armor weary, war yet won.

: :

And if our God is fair and just,
RESCUE one now rife with rust.

Deliver him from Lion's lap
if free the LAMB from tooth and trap.

pure speculation

known a few, if wingless yet
were clearly of an ilk

angel baby suffragettes
entirely of silk

::

somehow knew them right away
worldly they were not

many gone as earned their pay
I think of them a lot

::

dearest friends with open hearts
Christmas in their eyes

mortal foibles, human parts
but cherubs in disguise

::

heard it said that only kin
can see them, truly tell

does this mean that I am twin
to ranks of Raphael?

::

that would be a belly laugh
halo, feathers, me

anointed with His holy staff
an angel wannabe

: :

and still I ponder, mulling this
a seraph, maybe true

something in the way I kiss..
like sugar plums for you

rille

you kinda have to understand
how big it was

how big it is

moment when an acting student
cries in front of class
first time

lets it go, fear of looking stupid, scared
fragile, naked, ugly, wet

or withered
dim when tears refuse to fall as yet

                    : :

Meisner repetition drill
back and forth
to make you listen

bid you hear another's voice
than that which blisters
in your head
(the one that stays
the wail)

those who've taken classes thus
know wholly what I mean

my plan to blow up red balloons
blue and purple, tangerine

and jam them in imagined car

to bring them to a dying friend
who hasn't long to live

my goal

::

my partner with another task
both affixed with grit
each of us had
little time

ire, anger, *LEAVE ME BE!*
as tempests riled

her and me

::

my breath inflated more
and more
balloons like skittles
found the floor

it left my head too light
not right

I thought of who I planned
to think of
daydream of a stiff *what if*
emotively prepared

one I loved before who lives
then and now, within
my heart

(as doddering and plebeian
those last few words
do read in proof

no others seem more apt)

pictured him beneath
a blanket

heavy on his lightened frame
recalled an early Holiday when first
we were as
one

                    : :

Thanksgiving Day, some years ago
he and I and no one else

simple meal for simple boys
rich in what we had
(not much)

took a bag of gifts I bought
from discount store
the week before

and made him such a bathroom ball
frippery from wall to wall
he knew not for
the words

shower curtain Santa scene
fluffy rug of scarlet, green

matching cozy for the bowl
elf-and-sleigh-themed toilet roll

glass for toothbrush
reindeer noses

wreath on window, shiny bows

dish and soap with pine and berry
Christmas trees on towels, very

strung some lights across the ledge, over tub
round mirror's edge

recalled his grin, Noel revealed
door flung open, 5 & Dime
cheap like gum in
olden time

but full of Rankin-Bass

         : :

back in class, balloon at lips
determined in my whet
and hone to finish
what I started

here

quondam saved up
maybe years

         : :

there they were without a sound
rivered gush with victim drowned

tracks and torrents, dared not brush, need to
do this, have to rush

kept on blowing up balloons
to match the bathroom
Yule festooned

to give a friend a hued bouquet

balloons to send him
on his way

                    : :

and as the teacher brought us back
to where we were

attuned our tack

was very hard to stop the weeping
happy for the tears not sleeping

happy too, the fancied plot
imagined only

crying not

sparkle

without the dash, her flitter flash
minus gleam and glint

    held her own 'tween eye and lash
    for still I had to squint

glimmers glowed, her glitz, it showed
a brilliant bevy blazed

    glitter glaring, flame it flowed
    the fire quite amazed

               ::

twinkled stars, our flight to mars
luminous the sky

    as shimmers shined her avatars
    flickered when she'd cry

more than light, her ever bright
and razzle-dazzle blend

    beacons beaming burned all night
    an Angel 'til the end

Straight to Hell

(raging blaze adjacent lane)

Flaming lips
    meet quiet road,

last eclipse
    was last it snowed.

Nigh the foil,
    hot and cold,

frost and boil,
    stranglehold.

::

Give me fire,
    keep the freeze,

burning tires,
    Christmas trees.

Memories that
    melt the tar,

molten vat
    of icy car.

::

Driving fast
    as embers lick,

slowing past..
    Should take a pic?

Open window,
　　camera steady.

Open door,
　　the drama heady.

　　　　: :

Focus shot
　　as blazes climb,

worried not,
　　it's Wintertime.

Lights the lane
　　with yuletide glow,

the charred remains
　　of me in snow.

Thomas's guitar

warm pajamas, Winter night
   stolen moment, thought I might

borrow strings from brother's room
   play a song for him or whom

Mickey Mouse can show me how
   Paul McCartney I am now

fore I drizzle off to bed
   this I sing, no words were said

please don't see the sad in me
   only feel a Christmas tree

reflection in the shiny wood
   remember when.. I wish I could

Translucent

(after Church)

Squint your eyes and hold your breath
   as call to mind your favorite lake.
      Then wheel about to feel the breeze,
         come fly with me, a journey take.

Between the sun and chalk of moon,
   espy a cabin far below
      when breathe a whiff of Sunday ham
         as gliding on its fragrant flow.

Find our feet upon a path
   that leads us through an open door.
      Whilst empty grate, a fire glows
         and fiddle croons a lively score.

Though no one present, much ado
   with potent smells and laughter's peal.
      Sounds of feeding from the table,
         long-forgotten Sunday meal.

Silent whispers singing loud,
   bluegrass yodels, unseen choir.
      Bearded fellow leads the round
         in unfamiliar, late attire.

Bow is but a hickory stick
   for birds alighting, rhythm keeping.
      Child hums beneath his knees,
         stuffed as nodding, half-asleeping.

One can almost see the couples
  dancing off their two desserts.
    Doggies bay as bark and howl,
      seeing masters swing and flirt.

Out the window, boys that race
  for girls that cheer their wooers on.
    I look to heaven, feel the sun
      as down again and all are gone.

TWO FRONT TEETH

(horror, comedy, Christmas film)

Film I starred in,
yes I did,
more years on
am off the grid.

Recently
I broke a tooth,
appearing homeless
(near the truth)..

ONE FRONT TOOTH
until more cash,
I won't smile,
grin won't flash.

Still, I'm happy,
look like hell,
notwithstanding
ne'er-do-well.

Asks for nothing,
no regrets,
actor who
you'll soon forget.

If irony
ain't lost on you,
one front tooth
is less than two.

http://www.facebook.com/two.front.teeth.movie

welcome home

(Finland)

snow and snow
  and more in tow

chilly winds
  when blizzards blow

Winters, maybe
  all I know

drifts that wander
  to and fro

        : :

navigating
  streets is slow

snowball fights
  of scoop and throw

bright, the nights
  with frosty glow

Northern Lights
  an icy show

        : :

inside, mostly
  laying low

warm the cocoa
  make it so

remembering a
  long ago

Christmas kisses
  mistletoe

          : :

under white
  the flowers grow

Spring, when rivers
  overflow

but for now
  our status quo

grab your shovel
  here we go

when Mom forgot that I was gay

(senility as absolution)

"Why you cry, my Johnny?"
asked the Ancient Mother
of her Son.

"I don't know," replied the boy
as heard his name from
toothless lips.

Indeed, his words deceived.
A name not spoke in
many years.

Knew the WHY his tears welled up
while wet consumed
his sight.

And in that blur, those toothless lips
were hers, were young and
tinted Maybelline.

Food

Atelier

(how to zip up dress)

An evening ever long ago,
      couturier, a fashion show.

David Gold, the brain behind
      Kathy Reilly's dress design.

Johnny Saur sewing hem,
      on bended knee, at foot of femme.

Runway bound, our ingénue
      in fifties, strapless déjà vu.

Lemon lace with netting neath,
      silken corset, snug the sheath.

Bow to muse whose lips do utter,
      'Honey, please.. O where's the butter?'

chip

Artistic, autistic, feeler of all,
for good and for ill, the big and the small...

..wrote me some words, some call it a SCRIPT,
followed most rules as others I stripped.

Added some photos like books from my youth,
Christmas and frogs and fables, forsooth.

Added some links, some music I found,
songs for the reader, to gently surround.

: :

Added some musings, related asides,
on characters, plot... informative guides.

Added some bounce and bold to the font,
trying to make this a lyrical jaunt.

Kinda that's it, embellishments mine...
..rest was en pointe, me toeing the line.

Like watching a FILM all laid out for you,
my wish was to offer a magical view.

: :

Finished it up and proofed it like mad,
an imperfect thing all wrapped up in plaid.

Sent it to folks I knew in the biz,
smiled a smile, *"THEY'LL THINK ME A WHIZ."*

For how could one open a gift such as this,
delivered with love and sealed with a kiss...

..and NOT dive right in, eat up my prose
and poems within, I couldn't suppose.

: :

Waited for brood to give me a buzz,
email or text... *"A PARTY THAT WAS!"*

But weeks came and went when nothing was said,
as started to wonder, *"HAS ANYONE READ?"*

Reached out to more, to Facebook and friends,
determined as ever, me bucking the trends.

Replying, *"OH YES, OF COURSE I WILL READ."*
I mentioned was tricky and how to proceed.

: :

Preparing my peeps for what was to come,
the rules that I broke, the rhythms I strum.

"SEND IT, DEAR WOLF, I'M FULLY ALL IN."
Mailing the Script, not hiding my grin.

Again heard me zilch, except from a few,
"IMPOSSIBLE READ." How could this be true?

Sat in the corner, were brimful, my eyes,
weeks and then months as soul in me dies.

: :

Hoped it would make a film worth its salt,
instead, I begrudge, it's likely my fault.

Borne on my frame, a delicate chip,
lashing at friends, all strangers I rip.

Screenplay that lists LOVE as its core,
I shun all that meaning and simply abhor...

..helpless to rid myself of its weight,
chip on my shoulder seems fill me with hate.

: :

http://drive.google.com/file/d/18Ys7X4bp9aaxU3K4YHzfTP
5LECkQ-ZeR/view

CUP

Rid me of this dry-mouth dream,
O wet and warm with rising steam.

Wash the sand from corner eye,
cleanse me, caffeine.. purify.

Brewed or Instant microwaved..
my morning rescued, soul be saved.

Sugar crystals, saccharine dust
are neither nor.. more virgin lust.

No milk or cream as stirred with spoon,
all waxing sunlight.. waning moon.

Chalice lifted, first two sips
with heaven's brew between two lips.

donut shoppe

remember most the dozy lights
the globes that glowed
with tiny bugs

no more abuzz with life

little bones that gathered there
the bottom of the
orb

: :

recall the dirty vapored glass
the panes that begged
for finger words
and hearts
that

folded
yours and mine

: :

am lying here as thinking of a love that maybe never was

reflecting on that rainy day
across the booth and
there you sat

with powdered sugar
cherry lips

our sticky kisses cross the table

spilling milk
and spitting grins

sweet the jelly savor still

                    : :

no

the love it was

it is

eyes mirror soul

taste the frozen, let it melt
        upon your lips and tongue
remembering how first it felt
        when you and I were young

Summer days, the heat had won..
        its prize upon the floor
endless sweat in puddles, sun
        as night would promise more

recalling those who had no coin
        though remedy was known
the cool and sweet they could enjoin
        when bought an ice cream cone

you with yours and some without
        and may I recommend
forevermore and life throughout
        to look away, my friend

or not..

wet you feel that stains a cheek
        when sweat no longer drips
are eyes that thirst what heart will leak
        if given honest sips

and all at once you see within
        your mirror turns inside
and tears that fall from lips and chin
           are, heretofore, your guide

suddenly, with no regret
        when hot is minus cool
another licks your ice cream, yet
          you laugh.. a sweaty fool

Fried

Sizzled spits of

molten BUTTER..

Fizzled bits of

WORDS I utter.

Melted squares

of golden GREASE..

Felt the scares

of BOOK's release.

Pats that bubble

burn the PAN..

Vats of trouble

WORRY man.

Brown and serve

and buy my ODES..

Clown with nerve

IS BEGGING loads.

grease

unctuous rings of flesh and fat
pig bequeathed, all wavy flat

float atop the molten cheese
in hot and gooey calories

sauce and sausage add their sin
to crust baked tender, crispy thin

soonly sliced and divvied fair
wedges carved as cleaved with care

sharing seems the hardest part
this pepperoni work of art

pie makes men eat lunch alone
pizza slices all their own

http://www.youtube.com/watch?v=VoE7dUoL_9U

hors d'oeuvres

with hours prized
my verses short
and yet my ADD asleep
the words in tight corrals I keep

    even given lots of space
    as time enough, no want of pen
    each leaf I write of book or script
    is like a modest drop I drip

           : :

an intro, arc, and ending pure
(with tiny boat as short my moor)
maybe, heretofore, I think
my reasoning is clear (I drink)

    bored I get if faced with years
    writing one big hash
    so little bites I chew, digest
    it's finger foods I seem like best

           : :

taste I want, not dinner spreads
let others chew their drawn-out meals
(yet, assured, I've written tall
for munchies, tidbits add up, all)

    daily, makes for sated self
    longer still as bellies fill
    eat and read, I raise my glass
    to health as writing small, en masse

more delicious offerings
like onion blooms and fried-up cheese
ribs and wings and shrimps to dip
chips and guac and shots to sip

    I think my readers like these more
    than paragraphs of spinach or
    those bunless burgers writ too long
    I'll maybe add a psalm or song

            : :

rhymes to perk a stodgy page
I offer pause, for you engage
dribble words that leave your digits
greasy, needing licks

    and in the end you'll think I'm right
    dining here with me tonight
    and, please, I'd like to underscore
    my enchilada needs no more

Ice Cream Day

(a photo prompt plays havoc)

Saturdays were for Ice Cream. Today was no exception.

Maribelle, only half-awake, spent her first half-hour in front of the open safe (or as most people would describe it, the Manor's Fort Knox annex) deciding the color she'd tint that funny streak of white hair inherited from her Mom. Fully 10:17 AM, she pulled out the oft-chose Azure 24 highlight mix, the tube half-empty, half-wondering if blending it half-ly with Rose 37 might extend its life.. might make a pretty purple. A gutsy decision was made: Apply blue to roots, pink to tuft and tips, aiming at a mauve-in-the-middle ombre effect.

She closed the drawer filled with leaden tubes of dye, holding tight the two she'd soon squeeze. The vault slammed shut.

::

Opening the door to the closet too big for most girls her age, she knew exactly which skirt she wanted to wear. It was her Aunt Mary's prized dirndl from 1978.. three tiers of tiny, mismatched ditzies, the layers edged with glittery periwinkle eyelet. The blues and greens and pink sorbets seemed to lift off the fabric and would perfectly complement her hair. The fact it was Aunt Mary's *favorite* Disco skirt, its memories spinning out in swirling fabric circles under a mirror ball sparkling literally and metaphorically above, made Maribelle's choice easy. Under the bed's canopy, she laid the skirt on the satin duvet along with her favorite blouse.. a pale heather-gray tank top.

Perhaps there wasn't a lick of matching gray in the skirt, but she liked the way the top framed her pert bosoms, and knew the neutral shade would not steal focus from the pastel party swirling about her knees.

She paused for a swaying reverie, leaning shins into the bed for balance, finger lightly on chin, reflected fondly on her Aunt's back-in-the-day dancing exploits.. twisting round and under the arms of polyester-clad suitors as they whirled her about mercilessly through the manic machinations of the driving dance-hall rhythms. She could hear the throbbing strains of Euro-discographies forcing couples through endless variations of push and pulls, tilt and twirls.. just as Aunt Mary described.

: :

But it was Ice Cream Day.. and we all know what that means. She closed the door to the closet (or as most people would describe it, the East Wing of the Manor) and sifting through a mound of unopened, brand-new, six-to-a-pack panties piled high and nigh the bathroom door (as would rarely do laundry), she collapsed onto the chaise lounge facing the Wall of Mirrors. All these choices, selections, decisions had exhausted her.. Maribelle smiled at her image (she was ineffably yummy) and thought about Peppermint Ice Cream. Dye tubes, panties, tank top in hand, she arose as entered the Bathroom, Spa, Solarium.

Did I mention it was the Day to Eat Ice Cream day?

: :

The Limo was a little late. She had plenty of time to choose just the right pussy. Her tsar and darling Russian Blue, Leopold, seemed the least interested this morning, opting rather to sit in front of the aquarium (or as most people would describe it, the Manor's Grand Ballroom) blinking lazily at the equally taciturn guppies swimming behind the glass of the 372,000 gallon tank.

Not one to blanch from a challenge (*knew* she could convince her Russian Prince that she and he were destined to meet the day head-on together), the bait and switch began. She shook a wand of delicate feathers, bells on tangled strings and swept them aquiver across her saddle shoes.

Prince Leo came a-runnin'..

Maribelle missed the days when the Cadillac was driven by Humans. Though it was safe enough riding in self-driving vehicles, and quite efficient, throwing Gummy Bears at the head of a person was a lot more fun than not. But throw them she did, even if they landed on an empty seat. She saved the red ones for herself and Leo, but not too many.. for it was Ice Cream Saturday. She did not want to ruin their appetites.

On to the Studio.

::

Of course, Ice Cream could only be served after that day's re-creation of a Mel Brooks film. The Cosplay Gods chose YOUNG FRANKENSTEIN this weekend. She was looking especially forward to that seminal Teri Garr moment when, writhing and rolling in straw-laden, horse-drawn carriage-ness, she'd sing, *"Roll, roll.. Roll in ze hay.."*

And whilst the green screen was hard on her actor's instinct, she knew the Gods of Post Production & CGI would perfectly sync her to the black and white, silvery beauty of the original film. Feline Leo languished in the scene, hoping rather for an improv belly rub. Maribelle snuck one in. She rued that the camera's FOV left out her Aunt Mary's dirndl, but happy it captured her flattering cleavage.

(Later, the big, blue pussy was in rare form as Frau Blücher. His *"Stay close to ze candle, ze staircase can be treacherous.."* was absolutely spot on.)

Finishing their subsequent rendering of *"Putting on the Ritz"* left them ravenous. I dare say lyrics were dropped as their attention retreated again and again to soon-to-be-lapped-up frozen desserts. Very understandable. After all...

It *was* Ice Cream Day.

jelly donut

    goo and gunk with glop and gook
all drips and slips and slops

    squeeze the bulbous pastry, look
and see how sweet it plops

    mmmmm, I want this tasty bun
donut fried and filled

    to bite and sup, I've just begun
my tongue and teeth unskilled

                    : :

    for ever does the jelly leak
gluey lips and chin

    ooze the fruity sap doth sneak
squirting, staining skin

    then the center do I reach
its drenching stench of joy

    fragrance seeps, a juicy breech
as honeyed syrups cloy

                    : :

    fingers sticky, napkin stuck
little choice have I

    lick my digits, wish me luck
a yummy fix I try

puffs of powder mizzle mouth
with beard of snowy white

drops of jelly travel south
as sugar high takes flight

la difference

tween anthropoid and animal
twixt human being and beast
one is much more cannibal
on inner life they feast

food and fodder, bread and broth
can broaden neck and waist
whilst art and word, like flame to moth
a more acquired taste

found amongst the best of us
they offer pluck and soul
slice and dice, add gravy thus
and masticate it whole

roll your eyes, my mawkish rhyme
the verse is none but true
paean, music, paint in time
will fatten up your view

no legumes

bandishmental paradox
    for thou with whippet's bark and bite

accrudités, I gather lox
    to feed the beast a bagel, quite

the feat, his feet, or clory paws
    clumendous blankets fuzzied flam

tunely booned, yet broke no laws
    this thief of scarabolic lamb

ahh yes, the vaulted, faulted smip
    that endovars with hungry cat

their never-ending, grumpled grip
    (though one might, often, discount that)

left for thee no brunchly yums
    no dinnerisms, candle, desk

brutely chewed by varmint gums
    too little whit for humanesque

without, withinly, thinly crossed
    my pretzeholic yoga knees

coiled cracker, freshly flossed
    no foodinacious orts to please

so in completionistic barth
    I find the ending snoodly keen

garbanzo-lutely herb and hearth
    no fire bakes molassesed bean

not hungry

thought it unwise to ask for more

content with life and love
and lust, though last
that list, the lust

it must

did fall from grace and
lid from eye

a single lash
upon the face
of one she kissed

another time

when words could rhyme
and skinny was an
easy trick

no waistline thick

with fingers down her throat, she wrote
lithe, my lovely lean and lank

: :

that filled her tank with see-thru lace and swiss cheese holes of

gaps more lush than that which
held the slits and cloves
in place

cracks that grew to gulfs apace, bridged between
with narrow roads

travelled paths that led to reeds

reeds that led to bone
alone

: :

and looking back at what she lacked, had
no intent to feed the space

with anything
of worth
as
wan

with anything
to girth
a
swan

too dear the fear of overfill
vacuums left as rest would spill
no squeezing hope between her lips
less is more for slender hips

enough to eat
for one to
live

but never
nothing
more

to
give

olio

I know not how to edit when
my ink is thick with zeal

       through my fingers, out my pen
       a stew of how I feel

crabby carrots, cranky peas
taters stirred in poop

       fatty meat with grouchy beans
       cantankerous my soup

          : :

or otherwise, I shower praise
as sniff the potpourri

       all lavish flavors stirred for days
       and served with pleasant brie

never in the middle, dear
superlatives I spew

       grab your bowl and give it here
       as taste a rant or two

peanut butter

gooey, gummy, STICKY, THICK

CHEWY, GLUEY, take a lick..

Wonder Bread your JELLY PAIRING

SLICED BANANA, if you're daring

lapping knife or SUCKING SPOON

SUNLIT SNACK or light of moon..

to the cupboard, WORTH THE TRIP

MUST PROMISE not to double dip

reaching out to help a friend

(old Facebook post)

Is there anyone in the LONG BEACH, CA area with decent, unwanted furniture.

On page seven of my JELLY DONUTS script, a lovely lady enters the scene dancing to a YouTube video. Catherine. She is the gal whose couch I slept on years ago when first writing said screenplay.. and when homeless.

Of late, my new landlord has been.. well.. a douche. And I need to consider my options moving forward. I called the aforementioned dancing Catherine, touching base, exploring new/old possibilities.. with me, perchance, soon to be homeless again.

I was caught up on all her latest.

: :

The comfortable couch gracing her living room, supporting my then dreams, cradling my cats.. is gone.

Her building's manager had ordered several floors of tenants (most being low income and Section 8 recipients) to remove all soft furniture when a neighbor's bed bug infestation spread to adjoining apartments.

With one hard chair (and blessfully new cot), you might find her alone in verily empty room, perhaps watching old reruns of TWO AND A HALF MEN.. a guilty pleasure we shared loudly when together.

: :

A tad older, now unsteady on her feet, she still makes a daily trip to the McDonald's around the corner. Abhorring the food herself, will collect a friend sitting near the golden arches..

a different son or daughter each trip.

A *homeless* son or daughter.. one she never birthed nor hardly knows.. and treats them to a five-course McDonald's meal she can ill-afford.. sipping coffee as offering an ear and possibly advice when sought.

Then back to her bare apartment.

: :

I'm writing this on behalf of Catherine.
Most of you, my FB friends, know and love her, too.

As I am so rarely online these days..
please let her know directly

if, maybe, you could

help.

red

stabbed with stiffened Twizzler stick
    stale the stave, its sweetness stung

      left for dead as I did lick
          the tasty blade with tip of tongue

SWEET

Reflecting how, of late, it seems
I've twisted toward the shade.

       Now leaning nigh to yummy dreams
and orange marmalade.

: :

Gloom is easy, candy hard,
this caramel-coated verse.

       Syrup-seeking, honeyed bard,
in sugar.. will immerse.

: :

Toothsome treats to tempt the tongue,
your taste buds, I am toying.

       Pastry, pudding, pies among
confectionary cloying.

: :

Chocolate peanut butter cups,
no room for savored eats.

       Ice cream cones we lick and sup,
skipping sausage meats.

: :

Rainbow-swirling lollipops,
cupcakes frosted thick.

     Gummy bears and lemon drops,
enough to make you sick.

: :

Purest praline, pitted prunes,
patisserie with words.

     Teeth will rot and none too soon,
as butterscotch will curd.

: :

Clotted comfit leads to mold,
decay due lack of light.

     A foray short in sweet, behold...
am more at ease when write of blight.

tops in tubers

I heard this piece of advice years ago. Perhaps a version of the tenet is google-able. I don't want to check.

Always offer your GUESTS your finest comestibles.

Even if they are unaccustomed to such kindness, happy with more humble oblations —

never serve less than your BEST POTATO.

: :

For tomorrow, should another friend arrive for dinner, one worthy much higher regard — deserving far more pomp and circumstance — yesterday's okay potato will be, by default —

TODAY'S BEST.

And you will still be mashing, for this man or woman of great and noble import, your very best potato.

: :

Precept goes something like that — and maybe I wrote it silly. Perhaps the way I've explained it makes LITTLE SENSE.

But does to me.

As the season of my life nears with taters low to middling — KNOW that I offered you, all, my very best.

UNICORN TOAST

(Google it)

Creamy cheese
      with FAIRY DYE.
Sweetened fluff
        for SUGAR HIGH.

Cute enough to
      make you CRY.
Smearing bread
        'til BEAUTIFY.

: :

Charming as a
      BUTTERFLY.
Candy toppings
        MULTIPLY.

Viral versions
      HURT MY EYE.
Rainbow shades
        that HORRIFY.

: :

Woefully,
      I WON'T DENY.
End of World,
        might SIGNIFY.

Me, without
      my SAMURAI.
Weaponless,
        I bid GOODBYE.

Ever would I
      EVEN TRY.
Leaving one to
        WONDER WHY.

Crucial that
      I CLARIFY.
Eat that crap,
        I'd rather DIE.

Hieroglyphics

2 tomes

(vendetta)

new is life, a picture book
with annotated verse

old is plain, come take a look
as words alone converse

: :

words and words and words and words
space between them same

are syllables arranged in herds
domesticated, tame

: :

but 'tis the way it's always been
this older of the scripts

dare thee not to add your spin
might tempt apocalypse

: :

countless pages nary change
no rest for weary eyes

forward, backward, rearrange
no room to compromise

: :

of course your brain can conjure up
an image in your mind

of course you hear a tune well up
that words can help you find

                    : :

pray thee, why do thou protest
when author adds his touch

let it be at his behest
or does that spook too much

                    : :

allow the world to flex its wrist
allow a writer fail

but leave him be, unmake your fist
he fights against the stale

and still they bitch

you mock me for my RHYMING GAME
                'your jingle-driven odes are lame'

what the heck and who the fuck
                are you.. insisting SONNETS SUCK

self-exalted quill elite
                who taunts me for my STANZAS SWEET

harmonic lays of runic bliss
                as rhythm, rhyme and COUPLETS KISS

worry not, my vapid friend
                the how I choose my VERSES END

unworthy of the ink I leak..
                write your own, you POMPOUS FREAK

breakfast rune

zygote thoughts that drift and amble
mosey, saunter, stroll

over-easy musings scramble
shells add crunch to bowl

: :

I pick the chips that choke my maw
spit the shreds from lips

find a yolk of roe too raw
shuck of genius slips

: :

and yet I think my words are paste
no diamonds carved in verse

or maybe shards I chew and taste
are gems and not for worse

: :

likely somewhere in between
both will break a tooth

when be ye old or poet green
dentured quill or youth

: :

fear thee not your state of grin
crack and crush your ode

floss and brush, repeat, begin
let dental work explode

: :

take my bacon, eat my egg
savor rhyme and flow

leave my crumbled tusks, I beg
and read the me you know

dorian

(Wilde)

sometimes, I can't catch my breath
more like falling, squeezing
lungs and heart too
small to fit
the air

fit the dark and
ache and never, ever
fit the

: :

red that sweats from threads and pores
and corners of one's brimful
eyes as wrings the
wet with
tears

(so old those words)
all slowing, knowing, shrivelled stream that
leads a boy to

: :

die again, triptych verse of breath
and blood and paint
that ties the
tropes
to

brush, and canvas soul
that crumbles well with age when
stretched by frame

fret

I worry about misplaced commas, lines of poetry that get
chopped up by smartphones, awkward phrases
that didn't seem awkward

the first 6 edits.

I worry that my babies, my words, my verse
won't get picked up and coddled

for something I've
done wrong..

his brain was like mush

reading, re-reading
and reading again
fussing and fixing
leaving and letting

words he had penned years ago

his brain
like a sponge

one that had
washed too
many pots

sodden, unwringed

tomato sauce
pinking and
browning
its edges

likely to mold overnight

Inspiration

Step inside my secret lair
where motivation floats on air,

and stench doth mix with St. Laurent
— as experts reek of dilettante.

On page I smear a smirch of shit
I've scraped from hoof — manure and grit —

to offer you a slice of life,
a pinch of poop I've cut with knife.

Is stool to some, sachet to few
— delicious mixed with number two.

I pray it's pleasing stuff and such —
either hailed or not so much.

it seems

(narcissism)

    open Word... I'm all alone
praying for a guide

    shepherd, beacon, chaperon
fears now amplified

    cannot, will not, find the way
without a muse to point

    inspiration, lump of clay
dig beneath, anoint

    bury, smear, immerse myself
verses wander 'bout

    poem writ as if by elf
and through my fingers, out

One Wednesday

Tallied up the day's receipts,
    twelve began with one complete.

Hope-filled morning, early rise,
    plans were plotted, caffeine eyes.

Midday yearnings, thought I'd be
    more along than noontime me.

Afternoon of hard fought gains,
    thoughts of napping entertained.

Twilight musings..   How'd I do?
    Day feels like I'm nary through.

Evening, dinner, family, friends,
    midnight peal, one poem penned.

PAGE or PLOT

(made from wood or would)

    I think a thought, a basic plan
something I might say
    as inner, backwoods 3 piece band
with banjo starts to play

    recall the phrase *'forest, trees'*
woodland whole, the plot
    single cedars, nursing these
words I prune a lot

    make the page a perfect oak
paint with verdant brush
    canopy of green like smoke
misty leavings, lush

    storyline is swept along
by single-minded winds
    zephyrs each need separate song
treetops primed for trims

    arc and action fill the thread
seamlessly composed
    stitching limbs with pencil's lead
devil, details.. prosed

    down to this, I write for stage
with overarching flow
    plot stays near in gilded cage
each page I sharply sew

piling up of verse

a swelling
waxing, booming
string

of fuses lit with
love and

sting

      : :

I choose to
tie my mounting rise

with space
between

for breath and

eyes

      : :

to stay the choke behind
my word

for without air
I die

unheard

SAFE

Never scribe with words SECURE —
chary verses. Stay UNSURE.

OFFER UP a couplet stew,
RISK imbued — an iffy spew.

Raise your SWORD, lower shield
— unprotected THOUGHTS you wield.

Welcome wounds as salve your SCARS —
hide not neath your AVATARS.

Screed

Screenplay thugs, pray tell me all
     your doctrines big and tenets small.

Incidentals writ one way,
     headings, slug lines, font.. *"OBEY!"*

And yet these vary, ask a pro
     when he vows yes and she swears no.

Spacing one way, margins that,
     "I won't read this.. THEY'RE TOO FAT!"

Would that Shakespeare faced such laws..
     quill would never yield applause.

If so monstrous breach of rule,
     don't deem it script.. *"BUT READ IT, FOOL!"*

(This is one in a series rebelling against writing precepts.)

Secrete

Elucidation often grows
with optics blind, when eyelids close.

    Shutting windows, drawing shades,
    sunless silence, fluster fades.

See more light in blackened room,
no distraction, lumens loom.

    Umbra floods our thoughts with blaze
    revealing more with shrouded gaze.

Sleep can follow twilight, REM,
limpid dreams alive again.

    Wisdom enters lighthouse dark,
    knowledge stoked by nothing's spark.

SELF-INDULGENT

Oft you paint in blackened word
as someone praying to be heard —

LITANY OF MOANS within
a purgative and noisy din.

Some so poignant, writ with grace
— some effete, a paper chase.

Chicken Little's clues were plain,
SKY IS FALLING, feel my pain.

Like the boy in Aesop's tale,
limit cries to eyes — not pail.

TELL ME ONCE and TELL ME WELL,
wallow less, don't stay in hell.

Teach me lessons, help me cope
with trumpet peals that offer hope.

TITHE ME NOT to feel your ache —
ink your truth and trim your fake.

Simple Note to Self

(an author and his peers)

As often as you're viewed as gentle and sweet,
let them see you fixed and
formidable.

Allow yourself an unpredictable edge.

Be a force to be reckoned with.. honest and open with both
praise and criticism.. delivering the latter with love
and respect.. but also strength and candor.

With acumen behind your words.

Receive well the same
from others.

Likewise puff and pan yourself.

(Be the writer read
by writers.)

still

(its meaning)

Raising DOUBTS on verse before,
    backing DOWN on adding more.

Simpler word there CANNOT be,
    8 small letters (minus 3).

Poet's *but* or Proser's *yet,*
    OTHER druthers I forget.

LAYERED meaning, NUANCED shell,
    stops momentum, casts a spell.

All you've quilled in ink and gauze,
    comes a sudden PREGNANT PAUSE.

Calm and quiet REIGN until
    somethings written after *still.*

twilight query

what to do when day is drawn
now gleams its golden tooth

      still so much to write fore dawn
      a fractious time, forsooth

darkness beckons, take a sip
cruet spills its broth

      pen doth fear elixir's grip
      when ink ferments to froth

and all the words thou scripted since
the night and nectar fell

      next day read with wrinkled wince
      divining putrid smell

what Mari Beth said

(analogy of hourglass)

"your words akin to grains of sand
        a trio slipping through a neck

sieve adjoining bulbs more grand
        one by one by one, each speck

rather than an epic charge
        smithing sonnets, odes and tropes

squeezing wee as losing large
        with little lies and humble hopes

rarely do you plot a life
        defining brio birth 'til death

more, in fact, a sharper knife
        dissecting time as half a breath

ambitious tomes by lofty scribes
        are well-enough a touted type

yours advancing tapered vibes
        a stroke of quill and ink... a swipe"

thus a maiden spoke to me
        of staves I struggle daily write

tendered witness, ceded see
        my modest verse as small, not slight

writing

deeper still than dreamer's heart
    soul but scratches, shallow start

under thinking, neath a thought
    words and meanings quarry wrought

chasm, crater, cave unearthed
    down I dig, in dirt I'm birthed

catacombs and crypts I've searched
    hallowed ground that buries Church

sunken void, a plumbless pit
    pick and shovel, tales unwrit

quiller's grave with lode below
    drill I need for where I go

Me & Hue

altogether

I look around

and see
brindled bands of light
painting marbled stains upon my wall

tertiary tones and tints spilling out from plated glass
through the windows hind
my back

brilliant rainbows, prism-edged
leaded shadows there
and fielding
tween

::

I look around

and see
3 dead crickets, brief
their life, how they died.. unknown

and did they suffer when they passed and why
does God do so, this
thing

waxing sad as swept them up when
knowing they were
someone's
kids

::

anywhere you look

there's magic
everywhere there's pain
black and white and ghosts of gray

coloration, tinctured dyes wash away a neutral eye

see them all and if you
can, celebrate

the lighter
shades

asphalt jungle

(gumshoe sole)

Will cushion footsteps, scarcely make a sound..
like felted paws.

I laughed when first she left.

Knew she would recur, my prey, but nary knew the
where or whence... how fond she was
of animus.

Part animal,
all us.

::

Hair on back of neck would rise and tickle mane
and nape. So light and sweet, some nights.

Thought little of the dulling thud of boot on mortar..
mirrored well as synched with mine, her silent prowl dimmed.

Just shades of off-ness every few...

her radar likely rattled by my perfect profile,
silhouette, the handsome mien
I cut in black.

Even from the back, my bearing, something loathed
and loved.

How could she be exempt?

Ignored the stride that swallowed steps,
quick retreat when conscious of their own penumbrous pace.

Recall the eve I smelled her grief as wafted past my
lips and eyes and swirled about my nose..

made me laugh to think how
much she chose.

Never would I dream was there beside the curb,
behind her hair, when angled collar,
face and spoor...

cloaked as closed the taxi door.

Were growls heard another night, a moaning thirst
like injured curs, my females queuing up for damn to burst..

: :

Tonight at twilight, turned afore the setting sun
in glaze..

a face too nigh to miss, too far to find.

Too lost in amber rays too dear
to see the flash too near,
unclear.

Barely felt the contrail as it entered through my coat.

Hunter now the hunted one, brute brought down by beast.

It's true that time doth slow when ebon blinders fill our sight.
And still I smile mooning how she cared enough...

as sun and life are drained of red
in pools on inky
tar.

Their sanguine glow the same but for one momentary trice...

blood and starless beams of light
then lost in blackest

blear.

bipolar one

(in murk & pale)

pigments drift as wither way
the colder leaving warm..

BLUES that croon in midst of day
when not beset by storm

AMBER bookends blend their tomes
in pages, shades of gold..

sunrise, sunset leave their homes
as stories beg be told

here I live betwixt the TWO
an oddly-colored man..

twilight hides the strangest hue
tween indigo and tan

BLOCK

(of gay)

     would neutralize our rainbow globe
by painting us the same..

     these daubers missing frontal lobes
be humans but in name

     blocking splendor, boosting gray
their brushes smearing bleach

     you and I will slip away..
of color, we will teach

     canvas bare receiving stain
an easel dripping hues..

     palette mixing joy and pain
is ours to wield when choose

     blending shades on brilliant flags
chroma spreading truth

     bleeding red, our banner sags..
fixed at voting booth

BLUE

(van Gogh)

Moon as mist is thick as glue,
　　bleary stars in ragged queue..

Palette knife bedaubing view,
　　striping lake with flaxen hue.

Leisured stroll or rendezvous,
　　couple foreground passing through..

Away from crowded avenue,
　　to wander shoreline, night's milieu.

Vincent firstly praised by few.
　　When after death, his mythos grew..

Heart that ached for something true
　　bared moments bathed in woeful blue.

http://www.vincentvangogh.org/starry-night-over-the-rhone.jsp

CRUISING

spent the day, the afternoon —

having sex and washing
sox

for by myself was
having sex
with

— sox

                              : :

with self I did, and
maybe counts
or maybe

doesn't count the same

this sex with sox and self and —
palm and lotsa lube as
shot in tube

but sox got WHITE when washed them well, and hands got
SOFT from lube and gel — and wore those sox in

search of sex with other selfs at night

— their skinny jeans and
hipster shirts with
sox or not in
shoes

bar was dark as bars
are wont and I
did want it
dark

tonight

beard has gray
and yes tonight —
tonight I wanted young

yes, I wanted
young and BLACK with abs that only black men have
— HARD enough

to wash
your sox upon

: :

and shiny face and shiny heart —
to fill my own
for since
I left

the last I loved

my heart was left with
nothing left —

as left alone
to skip a beat with
little left to push between

and left me weary — leaning on the bar

ebon one, he knew the score

and door he opened halfway closed — the halfway
light on berry skin

and glowing teeth and
blackest eyes and
lips revealing

parted mouth
with pinkest tongue
that halfway showed his —

smile

                                  : :

night began when
knight began

removed my sox as BLACK man asked me how so bright
the cotton —

WHITE

led me easy to
his bed, and on his bed, and as we lay

how HARD he was — he really
was as asked me why
my hands

so
SOFT —

dusty colors

(tethered to balloons)

Honeyed tea and minty sage,
     cheddar cheese of certain age.

Lilac blended, splendid mix,
     blushing pinks with mallowed chicks.

Colors matte, fat and creamy,
     taste the fluffy, floating... dreamy.

Gather strings to lash a knot,
     lace with ribbons, soon forgot.

Drift amongst the cotton clouds,
     foamy seas above the crowds.

Filled with air of lighter net,
     words to write your novelette.

Tell the story, glory mine,
     fly aloft... a softer shine.

Ghostly me along for ride,
     holding on, forever tied.

gray

"he's but a jerk.. they should do this..
I have the answers simple as piss"

know that he's not.. know that they can't..
given your reasons feel more like a rant

: :

black and white thinking, true or false tests
never improve, no one impressed

more than your brain in front of a screen
thinking in snark, typing it mean

: :

those you call traitors, these enemies yours
some have been soldiers fighting our wars

elites that you loathe for speaking their mind
hating their words, turning you blind

: :

deep state as foe, swallow and gloat
feeling the bile rise in your throat

eggheads and experts holding a view
all of them fools.. when likely it's you

: :

everyone else has got to be wrong
never the singer, never that song

mosaic, the fix, blunted to keen
little bit dirty and lotta bit clean

: :

stop with the spit you spew from a throne
knowing solutions need whittle and hone

comments you spout, the venom you spread
read more than retch.. try learning instead

happenchance concert

was last and best of all the leaves
a brilliant scarlet red
when autumn offers, path receives
before me, where I tread

    eddy blew its helix whorl
    as settled, staying put
    attracted hues, this seed of pearl
    alighting by my foot

           : :

colors culled, at least be four
abreast the florid leaf
maybe five, perchance was more
I'll try describe them brief

    silent, stood, no longer ran
    found gazing as they grouped
    when bending down as runners can
    inspecting as I stooped

           : :

nigh, a crumpled pack of smokes
faded menthol green
it rivaled any elfin folks
with shades of tourmaline

    was by an empty can of beer
    bleached its royal blue
    regal mongst the pigments near
    the others by my shoe

there beside that crumpled tin
laid a ribbon pink
a birthday gift that could have been
and this, the missing link

    for next to that and north of this
    espied a glint of gold
    gilded chain a girl might miss
    her pendant minus hold

: :

with purple flowers close enough
the ones that make me sneeze
added lilac to the stuff
of chromas meant to tease

    blush of sun, be setting soon
    rounded out the cast
    whitened stars and silver moon
    above the hues, amassed

: :

not to mention moss and dirt
the bark of barren trees
dance of dinge, the dyes that flirt
with magic neath your knees

    symphony of tint and tinge
    let it feed your core
    these tasty crayons, free to binge
    are stories on the floor

Jars

(of comfit)

tasty, tempting, sugar rush

painted with a glucose brush

rainbow colors, blooming shades

stolen tints from six parades

chroma-coated m&m's

twizzler stripes like honeyed stems

day-glo skittles, keen and cloying

jelly beans, a fruity joying

smacking, snacking, sweetness sung

kaleidoscope on tainted tongue

dappled casts with candy 'neath

don't forget to brush your teeth

misfits

(rainbow found)

weird and welcome 'til were not
these uninvited hues

      lovely shades of umber plum
      and brilliant rosy blues

apricot with brightest pinks
one tangerine-y bice

      taupe and teal with luring whiffs
      of others strangely nice

palettes wholly impolite
the arbiters said, *"no"*

      banned from church and painted glass
      as left for rays that bow

who follow storms when herald sun
with arcs and colors mixed

      these blended hints of fabu tints
      and me, amongst the nixed

No Color

Color's lost when from afar

    or when I squint my seeing thin.

        All dots of gray and cloud and star,

            all soul and heart and eyes. No skin.

True for kites that fly aloft,

    true for friends we love below.

        Beauty blurred, all soothing, soft

            if color blind. Can see your glow.

PATCHWORK

(golden)

SINUATE and serpentine
maunder long a MAZY LINE,

    LOOMED FOULARDS on purled motif,
    floral jacquard HANDKERCHIEF.

        DAMASK set with cambric nap,
        toile and linen OVERLAP,

    SALMAGUNDI twisted lash,
    browns and blacks with SILVER ASH.

QUILTED thick like Persian rug,
fluted folds as FITTED SNUG,

    SHINY SLIPS of plaited tulle
    snake between the WEAVE and SPOOL.

        BIAS BINDING, silken thread,
        velvet flocked and LAID ON BED,

    COVERLET of eiderdown,
    neath bedizened... drowsy, drown.

Poem in a Poem

This rhyming thing is getting old,
    meter, rhythm growing cold.

Mindless lyrics sounding same,
    all endless beige, emotions tame.

I long release from rune and rule,
    no slave to words, this poet fool.

Is FREE VERSE where I need to turn
    as rhyming, rhythm bridges burn?

    A SHIFT in my soul's
    center gravity.

    Grabbing what shades
    and HUES I CAN,

    I scribble my thoughts.

    Backspace, deletion
    SELDOM
    as
    option.

    WHO CARES!
    It's fun!

    As learn to let go...

    no edits, no proofing, no worries, just SPIT!

So easy it sounds.
SIMPLE,

and
not.

I miss the undos.

Allow them WRAP COLOR
around my
stems.

Like hands might be holding,
both TIGHT and LOOSE,
flowers too
bright
for

fingers
and truth.

CRAYONS in BLOOM as rendered by one.

Above all quilled with little rhyme
        as rhythmless my petty crime.

Now spouting babble, yakking much,
          my posies minus odic crutch.

(Pablo Picasso – "Hands with Flowers")

ribbons red and blue

(patter, rhyme assay)

snaking from my fist
    arising out my wrist

        braided scars now almost healed

on heaven's waiting list
    but for artery I missed

        pain sequestered thus revealed

: :

another failed attempt
    at ridding my contempt

        turned the water crimson pink

as if I were exempt
    when oozing failed to tempt

        the spectre to the porcelain sink

: :

a measure of success
    no room for second guess

        end is near this time, I pray

in love they do profess
    with tourniquet compress

        they torture martyrs well this way

              : :

leave us be alone
    the answers are our own

        dare thee not to intercede

allow me find my home
    neath mound and marble stone

        please let the only lonely bleed

SOMETHING COLD

(untasty gulps)

A sizzling day in the SUN,
    our Summer had barely BEGUN.

        I sat in the shade,
            for breezes I prayed..

Some lemonade sounded like FUN.

       : :

I plotted the potion I'd FIX,
    my mind in the heat playing TRICKS.

        Designing the flavor
            seemed do me no favor..

With juices that no one should MIX.

       : :

Soon stirring my odious BREW,
    was downed in a twinkle or TWO.

        Thirstiness sated,
            my fever abated..

Aroma and chroma like GLUE.

stilettos

weaponized feet for hire
    armed below her knees

      with bladed heels forged in fire
        flaying flesh to please

    ::

blood as dye stains the pumps
    scarlet toes and soles

      fatal steps and lethal jumps
        will take their deadly toll

    ::

dominatrix, fetish whore
    for johns who worship feet

      naked, but for red she wore
        her shoes and sharpened cleats

    ::

always left a client spent
    grabbed her whip and split

      another nightly nonevent
        as wiped her mouth and spit

Top

(of steps)

Aiming higher, heading down,
  leap of faith or slip and drown.

    Choice is mostly (only) ours,
      how we savor sweet and sour.

Sorrow seasons everyone,
  nothing new as nether sun.

    That which differs you from me
      is what we do with what we see.

You see man alone on stair,
  I see climber, almost there.

    You see black of silhouette,
      I see light behind him, yet.

WATERCOLOR

C – rinkled, CRIMPED, creased and crushed
R – avaged, rendered rainbow rushed..
U – nder thunder, useless THREAT
M – y oh my.. but deadline met
P – resented to MY BOSS to please..
L – ots of laughter, third degrees
E – nds in trash all balled-up.. WET
D – og-eared artwork, pretty yet

water mingles tears and sweat..

world

(a case for humility)

abandon what you think you see,
      spinning globe, imagined strings..

tiny splinter, part of three,
      sea and rock and living things.

miles green of grass and plants,
      no détente with gods of fire..

swarm of bees and mound of ants,
      our souls don't place us any higher.

ort of dirt upon we sit,
      a speck of flying sand and flood..

swept along by wind and spit,
      far from ever grand, this mud.

here we live, this whirling stone
      with start and expiration date..

were we forged or maybe thrown,
      marble blue with Delphic fate.

Naughty

1978

Year of disco, best friend John,

hustle dancing, virtues gone.

Taught me moves, *seduce through jive,*

girls and whiskey, more alive.

Weekend blizzard, took the train,

zombies frigid, frozen brains.

City-bound in pointy shoes,

shiny shirts to hunt and cruise.

New club open, must attend,

trudging streets that never end.

Feet are cold, no mood to dance,

a chilly willy kills romance.

http://www.cbsnews.com/pictures/the-blizzard-of-1978/

BANDIT

Scruffy chin, KERCHIEF RED,
shoulders broad and Levi's spread

    atop his mighty tractor horse,
    shirtless, MUSCLED — stays the course.

         : :

Singing strains of JOHNNY CASH,
thinks he'll grow a mean moustache

    as felling trees and sawing wood,
    SINEWS GLEAMING — sure looks good.

         : :

Glowing pecs, his sweat don't stink,
STEALING HEARTS with grin and wink,

    outlaw handy with a GUN,
    never hanged — but maybe hung.

http://www.pinterest.com/search/pins/?q=farmboys

either

An enviable position to be in..

Choice I never dreamed (or hoped) for man like me to make.

Marina, dark with tropic skin, like guava split and spread and dripping. Ebon hair hid brow and eye.. whorling round her sun-kissed cheeks, dipping neath her shoulders tan.. licking, lapping 'bove her breasts.

Nipples broadcast heat and bother, begging me to touch.. to salve their pink and hard with lips, and soften stiff with spit and tongue as idle twixt the two, among.

A better use of mouth right then was not a thing I thought.

: :

But glancing at the other..

Jacob was a torso gold, blonde and buff of tall and lean, vee that stretched from blades to waist, beckoned glare and gaze below. Sinews raked from muscles firm.. rife with motion, even still.. rife emotion, seed to spill.

Even standing only straight with squeezing glutes as tensing thighs.. writhing, pressing, thrusting hips seemed ever throbbing, unremitting, back-and-forthing author's trance.

More splendid way to spend an hour quite escapeth me.

: :

And thusly, I went home alone. Neither, could I not say, *'Thee.'*

fecund

(by a one night stand)

costly the blunder, weaving her weft
presuming his horrible aim

> threaten and thunder, few missiles left
> leaving him tactical blame

'bite thee thy squeam, spineless you hold
blanks are the bullets well spent!'

> clearly her dream was fantasy bold
> not far was the trek that it went

alighting from flight, landed in dirt
clever the flying from gun

> nary her night nor luck in her flirt
> with only the shrapnel of one

Funnel Cake

(a sweet short story with ups and downs)

The dorm room was filled with the usual suspects.. skinny bed, piles of dirty laundry, Ikea desk, plastic milk crates, flat screen TV, Nintendo gamepad. An Excalibur poster shared wall space with a TINY PHOTO mounted behind a blue-green matte and black enamel frame. Next to that was a thumb-tacked postcard from Dollywood.

A rumpled, crusty TISSUE was suspended from that same tack.

BILLY owned up to his love of country music, but rarely his affection for Ms. Parton (or roller-coasters). Often found himself staring at the wall, melding these few guilty pleasures together in daydreamed trips to Pigeon Forge, Tennessee.

Wait. Have I described the photo within the frame?

: :

Simply put.. She was lovely.

MILA wasn't like most coeds. Yes, she adored boys and parties and spring breaks, but only from afar.. too reserved to start a conversation, accept a kegger invite, or plan a trip with friends to Daytona.

But FUNNEL CAKES were another story.

: :

The two met in the campus library.

Earbuds in, Billy listening to Ms. Parton's classic, *I Will Always Love You*, the decibel level must have been nearly precipitous.

Seated a full three chairs away, stack of tomes between them, Mila found herself UNABLE to sit still.. let alone study.

Instead, she began mouthing the words of Billy's favorite comely, curvy, country crooner using the end of her braid as a mic. Caught up in the fantasy.. had to rise, lift from her seat.. stand up and stretch her wings and fly.

From floor to chair to even atop the long, wooden library table.. LIP-SYNCHING for all she was worth.. Mila felt her cleavage deepen, imagined a piled-high, Grand Ole Opry wig balanced upon her head. Her silent miming now morphing into spirited mezzo-soprano.

She must have been *very in the moment*.. or the late-night library was particularly bereft of judging eyes.. for her usual, more tentative facial expressions (all shy about the metallics adorning her teeth) were enthusiastically replaced by full-on, AMERICAN IDOL lip gyrations.. perhaps hoping Keith Urban and Ryan Seacrest were hiding behind a pile of books and on the lookout for new talent.

They weren't. But Billy was.

: :

And there, that day, began the most glorious friendship. One that consummated in a trip to, of course, DOLLYWOOD. Her love of funnel, his quest for roller-coaster thrills converged on the buxom bosoms of Ms. Parton. That blithe spring break was *bucket-list special* for both of them.

Come fall, pursuing a newly offered Baking syllabus proffered by another University, Mila vowed to keep Billy and their trip close to her heart. He kept the strip of PHOTO BOOTH IMAGES taken that day.. framing his favorite of her alone.

'Twas a tiny frame, as noted earlier. The only one on his wall.

That Holiday Season she sent him a gift.

Along with a Dollywood postcard sweetly adorned with the cutest ballpoint holly and berries, was a one pound box of HARD CANDY, her C-plus midterm fruitcake exam, and a used, yet lovingly wrapped, Kleenex tissue smeared with but a swipe or two of FUNNEL...

..the petite chunks she wiped from her face and off his shirt, as our two descended that last loop of the Tennessee Tornado roller-coaster.. that delightful spring day in Pigeon Forge.

For nothing says MERRY CHRISTMAS like a bit of aged vomit.

: :

http://www.youtube.com/watch?v=hM6EUmOTkCI

Game

She stepped sprightly cross the chevroned slats, the parquet floor buffed to a high gloss. Twisting nimbly at the waist, lifting her right foot at the knee, she straightened the seam ascending her leg from ankle through calf to shapely thigh. Couldn't help but notice her reflection in the polished wood.

'Underwear is for pussies,' she muttered, laughing at both the obvious *and* parabolic natures of that phrase, smoothing the tiny leather dress that almost covered enough.

Adele was careful not to graze her stockings with the edge of her blood-red dahlia nails, fearing a run. It was not her place to do the rending tonight.

Happy she wore her closed-toe Jimmy Choo's as she had not painted her toes in two weeks, giving them a chance to breathe. No matter.. wasn't likely she'd remove her heels that evening. Caleb preferred they be kept on..

with precious little else.

: :

The hosiery was silk, the garter belt edged with eyelet. Whilst not a fan of panties, she felt naked without a thong de rigueur. But that, too, was how he liked it.

Nothing more than this but a corset.. nipping her waist, supporting now exposed milk-and-honey breasts, lording over melon-shaped buttocks when she spun around for his perusal.

He liked what he saw.

That night the safe word was evidently *'pussy'*.

Caleb seemed to say it a lot, albeit often in error.. instead referring to some finger food he was, at the moment, sampling. Knew it was a false alarm, she begged him not to stop.

He dallied with her pink hors d'oeuvres as nibbled on her canapés, lapping up the secret sauce.. supping soon the main entrée. From one set of lips to the other, he shared her almost piquant tang.. so she could savor, too.

Adele fairly wept, how good it tasted on her tongue.. holding the sides of the table upon which she, *herself*, was served.

: :

Dessert was topped with syrup so sweet, the whipping cream he ably supplied. Little was left on his plate, she grabbing it and licking clean.

He saved her bulbous cherry-on-top 'til very nearly last.

Her gratefulness was loud.

: :

He paid what he owed, settled the bill.. leaving a generous tip. As waitress, she was *nonpareil.*

She dressed in the dark as slipped from the room. Carrying her pumps to the circular stairs, she secreted down the ivory steps. Adele slid into the limo waiting forward of the manor.

: :

The sun had fully risen when stepping from the car..

She thanked the driver for his earlier, impromptu nightcap.

Removing her shoes first, tossed them unceremoniously in a corner. Off with the leather and satin and lace, and on with her sweats and tee..

and out with a can of Friskies Buffet.

Adele sat in her comfortable chair, feet up as surveying her kingdom. A modest room was all she needed. Gave the whore-money to charity, living on her nine-to-five.

It was the Game that she loved..

the Sport of owning men.

::

Bo-Bo, the youngest, wandered over first. He leapt upon as near her foot, settling in.. purring when she scratched his back with her still unpainted toes.

Stiletto followed soon after, licking his lips..

tuna was his favorite flavor.

::

Blew each one a tender kiss as hailing both her *'boy pussies,'* laughing at the pun..

the oxymoronic folly of life.

gorge

    Hall and Oates, they sang a tune
a lady of a sort

    who loved to make her lovers swoon
and break their hearts for sport

              : :

    late one evening ate a man
who wasn't fully-cooked

    wretched in ways I think I can
describe, as well I looked

              : :

    surmise she did not gnaw enough
nor marinate it right

    perhaps his flesh a little tough
I fear it wrecked her night

Hen Party

(Chippendales)

G – abby, Gertrude, GWENDOLYN
I – rma, God, she's too damn thin
R – ita, RHONDA, Rachel, Ruth
L – ola with the missing tooth
S – arah, Sophie, STELLA, Skye..

N – ancy NEVER did reply
I – asked them, please, to save the date
G – ina, well, can HARDLY WAIT
H – olly claims we never call
T – iffany, she HATES us all..

O – nly ONE is still unsure
U – ma swears she's too damn poor
T – o stuff her dollars down their TRUNKS..

whilst GRABBING at her favorite hunks

HIGHER HOPS

(SBDs)

There once was a bunny named BART
who supped on a carrot cake TART.

Was tasty as heck,
but tummy did wreck..

with hopping now fueled by his FART.

Our rabbit allergic to CAKE
gained altitude minus a BRAKE.

When started to fly
tween moon and the sky..

he noticed a whiff in his WAKE.

Bartholomew cyphered the SMELL,
a blending of carrots and HELL.

As silent the stench,
found brakes in his clench..

inhaling the stink as he FELL.

How Very Dare You!

I've NOT a clue why you and yours
    think me and mine have SILKY drawers.

NEVER thought the way I speak
    could smell of femme if GAY I reek.

It's HARDLY fair to judge the way
    a person walks when hips might SWAY.

Verily, I SHUDDER think,
    how dare you picture MINE in pink.

        That said..

IF you're cute and be the butt
    of jokes like this, I'll tell you WHAT.

With CPR, a hero true,
    and mouth-to-mouth.. I'll RESCUE you.

losing blood

Stiffened, thickened CURDLED CLOT
dripping from your nose like snot..

Give me CLUMPS of what you've got,
beseeching you to bleed a lot.

: :

Tasty trickles SEEP and SPURT
as bloody gobbets stain your shirt..

Embolisms hardly hurt
with OOZING BRUISES for dessert.

: :

Hardened cakes of JELLIED GORE
could make me want to eat you more..

I twist the knife and let it pour
and LICK THE DRIBBLES off the floor.

: :

Claret colored PINK CHAMPAGNE
from artery and gushing vein..

Next I GOBBLE up your brain,
methinks, perhaps, I've gone insane.

on the rocks

perfect pour of pure pristine
wet doth whet my wicked want
come and cure, to kill I'm keen
fight with fear and fume with font

    cold these cubes of cryptic cool
    sucking sips off severed squares
    licking love, this lonely fool
    plain the poet, pain prepares

      alcohol and after all
      wondrous words to wish you well
      vodka, venom, vitriol
      rhyming, raging, raised in hell

PICNIC

Blanket PLAID,
      her date with BRAD,

sure of what they ever HAD.
      IRONCLAD.

Dress was RED,
      he well FED,

was really quite the picnic SPREAD.
      Lots of BREAD.

: :

With it WINE
      beneath the PINE,

he kissed her lips as crossed the LINE.
      It was a SIGN.

Just as WELL
      as hot as HELL,

afternoon and kiss were SWELL.
      Love, they FELL.

: :

Ants, they CAME
      and had no SHAME,

though she tried to take the BLAME.
      A lover's GAME.

Crept and CRAWLED,
      were very SMALL,

as drank their amber ALCOHOL.
      WHEREWITHAL.

: :

Have you HEARD,
      is real, my WORD,

they chawed our twain with cheesy CURD.
      Seems ABSURD.

Voulez VOUS,
      this verse is TRUE,

had their cake and ate them, TOO.
      Ants WITHDREW.

plug

to trigger thirst for all that is
tween pages of a tome

self-promotion, boosting biz
without belabored drone

: :

adjuring mob to credit skill
yet skittish to implore

if beg too much, is overkill
attention-seeking whore

: :

balance, key when urging folks
"please buy my lovely book"

push too hard and, holy smokes
will never hazard look

: :

careful when you're squeezing eyes
resist the lure of bold

tread lightly lest they mobilize
a horde of uncontrolled

: :

readers hating what you sell
as well enough they should

rope it in and stay the swell
less is more... is good

: :

or not and scream your words aloud
deriding how they run

talent found in standing proud
persuade them with a gun

quill

(note to self)

Tipped with poison,
venom barbed,

hateful words in
lovely garb.

: :

Sweet intentions
sharpen verse,

soft and fuzzy hides
the curse.

: :

I demand that
poets be

more like whisky,
less like tea.

: :

Once you steep your
dulcet brew,

shake with bitters,
shock me new.

Roller Coaster

DIPPING, SLIPPING whiplash turns
summer sun on seat, it burns

GRIPPING, SIPPING, TIPPING drink
soda spills as rise and sink

QUIPPING, CLIPPING friends with goop
cue the spewing, loop-de-loop

LIPPING, DRIPPING chunks I blow
vomit lands on folks below

WHIPPING, FLIPPING bird at me
hurling, heaving, flying free

RIPPING, STRIPPING, zip off clothes
spray us down with fire hose

semblance

dispossessed of polish, shine
   snorting at a joke

entered bar neath Exit sign
   when came in from a smoke

oblivious of all the eyes
   that followed all the wares

skirt too snug made snug their flies
   her breast and butt affairs

: :

swilling cross the sticky floor
   to sit on sticky stool

the dive was better for this whore
   each dick a bulging tool

I dropped a dime, the jukebox played
   and six were on their knees

pled and pressed and plied and prayed
   to tango with our tease

: :

went out upon the blackened wood
   stained with piss and beer

rebuffing all, alone she stood
   beckoning me near

tossing waves of golden hair
    when wriggled straight her hose

tight her blouse, on cleavage stare
    as song and rhythm slows

: :

then opening but one more snap
    revealing one more bend

her curves between were like a map
    below, my journey's end

shimmy shaking, throbbing thrills
    her quiver quaking nods

jiggly parts that gave us chills
    further swelling rods

: :

took her hand as heard a moan
    when grabbed her round the waist

game we play to claim my own
    bar we danced, erased

damned we were, eternal life
    my succubus from Hell

darling, dear, forever wife
    beloved Jezebel

Sock 'em

Fury, ire, bile, rage..
    rarely check my anger gauge.

Censor, edit, yield confused..
    wrath released if undiffused.

Easy laugh means easy spew..
    quick to grin, can cry on cue.

Heart on sleeve with poison mouth..
    venom travels swiftly south.

Fists are formed as fingers curl..
    eyes that flash and daggers hurl.

I'll kick your fuckin' ass, you see...
    call me not your enemy.

toxic

her goulash, stirred with angry bites
an olio of bane

blackened eyes and bloody fights
a soup of acid rain

served in bowls of poison oak
ladled with a knife

no one supped and nary spoke
fearing for their life

: :

I alone did venture taste
mélange of steamy bile

delicious was the choler laced
with tiny bits of vile

ravenous, I sipped each drop
and savored every chew

seemingly I couldn't stop
until my face turned blue

: :

breathless heaves of throat and lung
left me torpid there

paralyzed, my soundless tongue
screamed a silent prayer

grinning, she didst fill my bowl
with more, her evil stew

laughing at my leaving soul
'tomorrow, made with you..'

UNDEAD LOVE

(broken hearts and other things)

There once was a zombie named Billy
who lusted for un-zombie Lily.

Although just a girl,
  not part of his world..

   still, Billy did eat Lily silly.

The story goes further, I fear,
when placing his penis in rear.

And tho it fit nice,
  it came at a price..

   left willy in Lily, I hear.

Realm

ALLEGIANCE

I've only lived inside
myself

I've never felt the sum of
you

no reason to believe your
words

if whispered slurs uniquely
true

::

and still I hold to distant
hope

these gloomy truths might errant
be

a quickening of spirit
sucks

the milk of orphaned
pedigree

::

no flag above me flaps and
flies

no rooted soul can feed a
fool

but only I can raise the
cloth

while others blame the golden
rule

: :

so if and when I make the
case

for forward sharing, wearing
grin

swear allegiance to the
one

who offers you what might have
been

American Pie

Strength is folded, baked within,
        is born unsure with fear its twin.

Bluster bears a fatal flaw
        for home and nation built on straw.

Balls of brass and swagger boast
        a bully pulpit's gutless ghost.

Quiet courage harbors doubt
        like humble pie with whispered clout.

Recipe to heal divides..
        an open ear to hear both sides.

Choice is down to fail or mend,
        if break in two or choose to blend.

http://www.youtube.com/watch?v=OPvVx9q-4NQ

BARN

(below the brume and blue)

Fast, the night that ever seeks
  to blanket land BUT NEVER SPEAKS

in verse, preferring mumbles slurred.
   BLEEDING LIGHT from yonder blurred.

Wreathing cotton stitched aloft
  interlacing ZEPHYR'S WAFT.

Whispers barely lit and still
   TWINING FLEECE in heaven's mill.

From dusk to dim to dark I see
  when stars illume the WORK OF THEE.

Your never-ending loom in sky
   WE SLEEP BENEATH, you labor high.

Barn and pasture pay a debt
  as workers spinning CLOUDS WILL SWEAT.

Quench our thirst, the land is owing
   FOR THE RAIN when overflowing.

Early shift with lanterns off
        in sunlight lucent, MORNING COUGH.

Whiff of smaze and vapors misting
        KNITTING NEW these billows twisting.

Painted red as echoes dawn
        between the rays and wood IS DRAWN

a morrow under welkin's puff.
        WOVEN HAZE and sun enough.

blame enough for all

soul who asks me for forgiveness
leniency and grace

I will...

he or she of either angle, big or small
first or last, gerrymandered

politician...

be the one who says I'M GUILTY
what I said was laden fake

and could have made
a fragile mind

rise up with this false revolt...

: :

be the one to say the words that
heal our State, our Country

World...

speak to those who eat their own
DEFY all truth when

spread their rot...

civility, it must return
facts cannot be heard above

the guile that inspires
harm as nothing

grows in
myth
and lies

fraud and fables strangle peace....

: :

both sides say it, SORRY please
for pointed pencils

pointed words...

your double-sided
saber-bladed, fore and aft
will stab you

back

BRINKSMANSHIP

bluster sown

      testosterone

why, unknown

      bloated clone

battle zone

      surveilling drone

Achilles' shown

      cover blown

blood and bone

      lying prone

empty throne

      headstone

by design

presupposing links were laced
and trammel fences, palings braced..
wall to keep the others part
of not to where he graphs his chart

    mortar knitting barb and stone
    agglutinating credo sown..
    precept lent to theorem's pitch
    whilst dogma marries faith to bitch

I believe behest decreed
with fundamental's edict freed..
broken down, assembled thus
not an option we'll discuss

    that which I pretend to spill
    and that which gloms on glove at will..
    reading this to feel the throng
    cannot abide our Sturm und Drang

hedged by wire, House of White
leader cowers oft at night..
bounded by the fringe who gird
and those who count as base and herd

    fairy tale of fractured few
    elected by a splintered coup..
    Nero fiddles, Roma burns
    pray to God a nation learns

Center

Too extreme, facing left..
  immigration, homeless, theft.

Pivot blindly to the right...
  climate's fine, guns, pro-white.

Somewhere in the midst of all,
  pundits cry on wailing wall.

Folks like me who seek some truth
  are offered scraps at polling booth.

A little this, a pound of that,
  Republican and Democrat.

Compromise ain't nuthin' bad
  unless you live in Leningrad....

http://www.youtube.com/watch?v=S65jqrHQi_c

crescendo

higher, holding firm belief
    if not without some sway

steady, still I move like thief
    to steal above the fray

silent secrets, parted lips
    louder spills my word

forward, toward full eclipse
    with sounds too seldom heard

bang on drum 'til blown apart
    cannon backed, the slog

cover ears and open heart
    when rout the demagogue

live too fast and ever woke
    let your noise be stirred

scream your whispers 'til you choke
    as roar thru life preferred

Finish Line

when circle fits the SQUARE
and DREAMERS fear to dare

when June and MOON are hung
as NEVER spoke nor sung

: :

when POETS can't compose
their KING bereft of clothes

when PARENTS forced to choose
at border wall, we LOSE

: :

when actors, ARTISTS be
REVILED for how they see

when SCIENCE now a joke
as climate up in SMOKE

: :

when ENEMIES of State
are those who love to HATE

when nation lead by FEAR
our FATE is ever clear

: :

when families are SPLIT
my side RIGHT and your side shit

when CHILDREN hardly grown
can brandish guns, seeds are SOWN

: :

when lies no longer STRANGE
when NUMB to all this change

when TRUE, these words, my friend
beginning of the END

God Bless America

"Straight home.. or they'll take you too."

Less a threat than heartfelt plea rooted in fear.. had already lost a Sister and Brother-in-law, couldn't bear losing his Niece.

For her part, she learned to embrace the shadows and come straight home.

::

It began like so many immigrant stories.. fleeing untenable conditions, seeking better.

Parents praying for a way out, path to somewhere safe, welcoming. It would be years before they could legally enter the US, paperwork tied up in bureaucratic knots. Maria was eight months pregnant.

Region's escalating violence, rise in child trafficking, drug cartels and gangs moving in.. their time to flee was now.

An arduous journey, to be sure, the smuggler was not at all like what they heard.. what they feared. He took great care to see Maria, with child, shepherded across the Rio Grande with her own handler.. a local lady who had helped Mothers and children before.

Baby was born premature the night they crossed the border. They named her *'America'*, maybe hoping it would bring her, and them, some much needed good karma.

Maria took ill, a casualty of the trek.. stress, lack of food, water, clean blankets. By the time they found a motel and doctor, she was already well past fever. Never again to see the sun.

The tiny town's church agreed to bury her. The ceremony held in tandem with America's baptism.

: :

Father and daughter found their relatives in New Mexico and settled in. There was a surprising number of jobs to be had without a green card.. though, all of them beneath Josef's skill and education.

Grateful nonetheless, he began working days in local fields, nights at a factory.

America grew up fast, learned not to volunteer, to stay quiet about her homelife, make excuses with the teachers.

She excelled in class, allaying any need for school to intervene.. no need to meet her Dad.

: :

The ICE raid at her Father's factory netted him and several others. He never made it home that morning.

How to tell a child: *Soldiers took your Dad.*

: :

Colder that Autumn than she could recall, she came straight home like her Uncle ordered, running past the homeless folks living under the bridge.

Some in school made mention most of these were Vets..
men without a home, returning from where they fought.

She wondered if any had been Soldiers the night they arrested
her Father.. wondered why they always slept with empty
bottles near. Often prayed they'd keep their eyes closed, not
notice her brown skin. But sometimes prayed.. just for them.

Nights were getting chilly.

::

Her Cousins worked some of the same fields her Father had,
after school and weekends.. coming home hungry and tired.
Complaining of cold feet was an oft revisited grievance.

America had an idea.

She helped neighbors with chores, walked their dogs, raked
and bagged piles of leaves, bought them their lottery tickets at
the corner store. Saving her pennies, gave half to her Aunt for
food.. the other, hid in a box under her bed.

Tuesday before Thanksgiving, she rode with her Uncle to
Walmart.. bought the biggest bag of fluffy, white socks
they sold, some crinkly tissue paper and spools of silver and
gold ribbon. What she didn't count on was, as luck would
have it, the socks were on sale.. three packs *(36 pair!)* for
the price of only one.

That night she painstakingly wrapped small bunches of socks,
sparkly paper between each pair, tied and bowed in the
brightly colored cording.

Tucked 3 bundles under her pillow (gifts for her Cousins on
Turkey Day) and the rest in her backpack.

With only half-day school on Thanksgiving Eve, America turned the familiar corner on her way home.

Instead of her usual running past the Soldiers, the Vets, under the bridge.. she slowed to a stop.

Shaking...

she opened her satchel and walked over to a man lying in the cold, open sun, leaving behind a small parcel of white cotton.. festive and trimmed.

Then again to the next, gaining confidence..

Now, not shying away from those awake, she handed out her treasures with a smile and a blush.

"Happy Thanksgiving," whispered America.

: :

Cried her way home thinking of Dad, a Mom she never knew...

as prayed the socks
were warm.

heroes

(resting Arlington)

    what is this we sing.. respect
for those we hold on high?

    showered praise, acclaim bedecked
receiver asking why

        : :

    so often those deserving most
can live no other way

    shy from cheers, are more engrossed
remaining in the gray

        : :

    tally up a legacy
with fans but keeping count

    no time they.. to oversee
the bottom line amount

        : :

    in the moment, in the game
where peers are seldom kind

    rushing forward, toward aim
their fears be deaf and blind

        : :

something human they possess
as something most have lost

deep they feel when others less
our lack of Robert Frost

: :

grant me, Lord, the strength to act
living pure as these

in marble etched, I make a pact..
stones beneath the trees

IF I BELIEVED

Add up years and minus luck,
    spirit drained as soul is stuck.

Autumn decade facing snow,
    frosty clouds hide hurt below.

Future closer, past unclear,
    viewing death through pained veneer.

Worry comes like missive penned,
    ascend above or hellish end.

Wouldst thou want to make that bet,
    leave this life not paying debt?

Let me lose this lust for night,
    bathe me, Father, neath your light.

Raise up eyes and welcome fate,
    take the plunge before too late.

Baptize thee neath seraph's sword,
    or risk thy dying uninsured.

Leftovers

Glasses off and squinty eyed,
    I spin around as wave goodbye.

Motion blur with double take
    in glaring light...   am wide awake.

Yet, I'm dreaming different life
    of film noir and bloody knife.

Black fedora...   loaded gun,
    a sable world I stripped of sun.

: :

All around me spirits prowl
    with smoky visions...   whiff of growl.

Night is filled with movie scenes
    and shiny streets on silver screens.

Let me play amid the past
    as dreams I conjure seldom last...

If remain, aroused they stay
    to drift like mist throughout my day.

loyalists

would that same befell on thee
on us, our storied land

    find oneself in need to flee
    a Civil War unplanned

triggered battles, woke the sides
dividing Clan and State

    brothers clash, our Union slides
    civility to hate

: :

and what of those who take no stance
with views averse to strife

    found in way of armed advance
    threat upon their life

begrudge them for their lack of faith
that neither side is good?

    hang them high as traitored wraith
    shun their doubt, we should?

: :

or bid them run like they who try
from neath our southern wall

    in caravans these quislings die
    freedom bound they crawl

"yes, fend thyself and fly thee north
keep your children near"

    seeking bastion, venture forth
    their status now unclear

            : :

taught, we were, protect our own
one Nation 'gainst the rest

    needing help, our cover blown
    now uninvited guest

refugee as fugitive
Trump has schooled them well

    "for aliens who ask us give
    assist.. deserveth Hell!"

            : :

when wedging shoe on other foot
they fail to feel the squeeze

    honestly, indeed hard put
    to pity bended knees

except to say they're filled with grace
brazenness and chaff

    and if observed they might embrace
    the urgency to laugh

            : :

Canada, their borders closed
no one let above

allowing entrance well-opposed
endorsed with Christian love

asylum nixed for all who pray
no mercy on the dregs

"we'll build a wall," Trudeau might say
to anyone who begs

most often

Nihilism seems to be
      the FAVORED FLAVOR of the day.

STATUS QUO suppressing thee?
      Destroy the Earth, rebuild from clay.

Problem is that ONE WHO KILLS,
      bestills his New World Order crave,

is bidden by the Fascists filling
      void, EMPLOYED as shackled slave.

New Parable

I can just picture Jesus attending that now legendary Wedding at Cana.

And shortly before He turns those jugs of water into wine, whilst still milling round with other gladsome gala guests, spots a lovely Sapphic couple with their precious little boy.

He's drawn to the wee one who might be playing with centerpiece flowers —

    picking one special for Mom #1,
        one equally pleasing for Mom #2.

Jesus wraps His arms around the little boy's shoulder, whispering words to the soon-charmed child.. *How blest he is to live in such a family filled with so much love.*

Doubtless, then, He speaks to our little boy's two Moms, offering His prayers that they remain so joined, bound and pledged, so welcoming of heart — to always be a home, as happy — as they are today.

Thereupon, I posit, our dear Lord would feel a burning urge to move and mix His sandaled feet (likely with Beloved John) to the rich and ancient psalm and dance the Wedding Band was playing —

    I'm imagining a Tom Petty tune.

http://www.youtube.com/watch?v=s5BJXwNeKsQ

parchment

(Varun's tale)

When dragons ruled and
spectres vexed

(their mischief deemed quite
    commonplace)..

there rose a VILLAGE blest
and bonny, not too far
from here...

         : :

high upon a craggy tor,
protected from the largest
    of the fire-breathing beasts.

An awning made
of rock

all but hid the
GRATEFUL town and kindred.
Folks, beholden, felt
quite safe.

         : :

   The reigning princess
ruled with GRACE

(lovelier than any kingdom's
daughter, ere or since)..
walked amongst the
cobbled lanes

often barefoot,
   ever HUMBLE...

ever giving comfort to the
woefully without.

             : :

A DAY like any other day,
except this one was
   not at all a
day like

all the rest.

On bloody knee, HE
fell upon afore
the feet

of princess fair.

             : :

*"I've one request,
you read my SCROLL.*

*I wrote it, please,
to change the
world*

*(as I avow he
   spoke the TRUTH)..*

*and you, a princess,
might know kings
and queens*

who'd read it,

make it law...

   proclaim the vellum due decree.

Bidding us and all who
serve..   listen first
and spread the
word."

                    : :

When henceforth came a
goodly bond tween
REGAL and an
INDIGENT

(with beggar's knees and
empty quill..

   and eyes well-filled with wet and hope)...
an earnest PRAYER for PEACE.

                    : :

Indeed, his LOVE went
round the globe and
touched a million
hearts and
souls.

LOST in time
   with words UNKNOWN,

our he and she
and SCROLL

on throne.

REFLECTING POOLS

Vapors hidden in a mist
where spirits mingle..   coexist.

    Something like a cry unseen,
    raindrop-veils with wails between.

Watch them walk amongst the warm,
crumpled zombies, often swarm.

    Dusty bunch who miss their view,
    different skyline..   déjà vu.

::

When towers stood with clouds and sky,
people worked in buildings high.

    When planes flew dreamers, safe their trip,
    never crashed with marksmanship.

When river mirrored many hearts
with blended views, September starts...

    Echoes of a melting pot
    now twinned, their fog with smell of rot.

http://www.youtube.com/watch?v=ivgTiP55psU

switching stations

(2018)

Limbaugh breakfast, juice and hate,
the wad of lies he'll masturbate.

FOX at gym, their sound on mute,
spewing fake while skewing truth.

Radio when driving home,
point of view is not my own.

Changing channels, TV spots,
pundits heaving, gushing lots.

Mark Levin, an evening chore,
flipping facts and flapping jaw.

Above conclusions solely mine
as no one asked me, still opined.

Friends keep close, your foes more nigh,
hearken both is what I try.

When they cross a bridge too far,
will turn the dial...   NPR.

Wanderer

Funny, LIFE..

seems evident one day, NEBULOUS the next.

Felt for the train ticket sticking out
my breast pocket, where men
used to show off fancy

silk squares.

::

The caboose was empty,
I relaxed...

a EUPHEMISM for me taking up
3 seats, 2 tray tables,

restless legs
stretching out full length,

firmly planting naked feet
on the armrest..
diagonal

cross the aisle.

::

Recalling the ever so TRUCULENT
Diner Car attendee....

"You want a cuppa WATER for what?"

Tried to explain my yearly trek..
HOLY pilgrimage, really.

"For Mr. Peepers...   I think he's thirsty."

The train rounded a curve,
throwing me off–
balance.

In an effort
to steady myself,
upended his
tip jar.

He SCOWLED as I left the car.

: :

How do you tell someone
of the SORROW...

losing your
wife,

taking care of her ridiculous parrot,
who will likely outlive you
and your children..
and maybe

theirs
too.

But I made her a promise.

His cage beside me, I TOPPED OFF
his water dish,

scratched under his little beak,

way she taught me..

: :

Visited her Parents each Fall. Now kids in
college, just me and Peepers,
3 States away...

The EXPLOSION of sadness
began at the station
the moment
I arrived.

Slow-motion crash,
stillness of SUFFERING,
year after year...

"..you seem fine, kids good?"

: :

This trip to Mecca, a few miles out,
late afternoon swirling behind,
I opened the caboose's
rear door.

Clickity-clack,
warm wind in my hair...

let the BIRD free.

: :

Forgot my shoes
and followed his lead,

flying..

Similitude

about to jump

lunge or learn to
live atop
the diving board above

precipitous the
lofty drop
avoiding those who shove

: :

brave who crave it
on their own
with nothing underpinned

leap as leave your
comfort zone
throw wary to the wind

: :

love and life
require us
to climb the ladder rungs

never stay upon
it thus
as never speak in tongues

: :

loud we shout if
bounding off
when blunt the language be

tell me what you
see aloft
and bid me dive with thee

http://www.youtube.com/watch?v=Rx0mYN32Kps

bangs

and even if unwise, you trim the fringe with
tiny snips

until you have no hair, no words.. no trace of
verse is left

and hit 'undo' a thousand times to find the root,
your roots again

Braid

(and haircut)

A PLAIT of hair
could lose its home
hanging from my neck.

Foot long twist
of blond and brown
with silver-crested FLECK.

Like a ROPE
around me drawn,
stiffened, fixed and set.

Self-imposed,
my ALBATROSS,
a levy for my debt.

::

Free me from
this fluted WEAVE
well-hidden from the light.

Slip of scythe,
sequestered view,
a new man OVERNIGHT.

Cut it off with
SCISSORS clean as
rest give proper brush.

Waste no time,
THE RECKONING
demands a fearless rush.

circle

bricks are laid from end to end

    as marble slabs, straight no bend

grout begirding polished dome

    cambered peak of golden gloam

glistens off the vaulted sides

    unseen edges, gypsum guides

blocks enfolding arc and curve

    purview hides what eyes observe

only gleamings orbit spire

    glowing steeple, twilight fire

adhan heralds call to prayer

    spheric turret made from square

http://www.youtube.com/watch?v=SSyEpZOsJNk

Cracked

Catherine's dish from cross the sea
in old-world, delft blue filigree.

Glued and glazed, its porcelain chips,
I fondle cleft with finger tips.

Once in use is now display,
a life ceramic in decay.

Might have held a potted plant,
but water leaked through fissure's slant.

Likely carried dinner's weight,
is little left but broken plate.

From serving supper à la carte
to maybe now.. objet d'art.

Metonymy of saucer curved,
as riven vessel fixed, observed.

Marveled at in mended glory,
wonders, all, its mangled story.

EYES THRU GLASS

windows have the power
mastery of air, life, hope

closed room, open sky
breeze between the two

feel buried when without them
as if were breathing dirt

drowning, caged, tho minus bars
prison up to lips..   and rising

hanging crooked

the curtain dips, leans to right
stanchioned screws are loose

and though it threatens, fall it might
we've come upon a truce

: :

he will stay and shield the sun
at apogee of day

I will gently stir his spun
when tucking drapes away

: :

away from opened pane and breeze
drawn for evening's gloom

away from rain and moonlight's tease
drawn for naked whom

: :

whom is me when sole within
the walls that line my cave

faithfulness doth underpin
as cloth belies the brave

: :

careful as I am, my friend
cautious with this veil

come to love its bias bend
curtain rod and errant nail

impaired

(RCA)

forlorn, the pooch who could not hear
the harmonies she urped

    when out the cone that boosted ear
    was deaf to lilt that chirped

        : :

an irony of life, très cher
could not perceive its worth

    from opera's hymn to shape, her pear
    her pair.. I shared his dearth

        : :

with deafness as a metaphor
for what is gay in me

    the song I miss is more her lure
    all beauty that is she

        : :

an aria of tiny waist
o'er hips of blended curve

    her sweeping strings oft open-laced
    with breasts she'd freely serve

        : :

legs that sing as promise squeeze
upon stiletto heel

    lullaby of lips that tease
    when frequently would kneel

        : :

the dog and I, indeed, akin
as silent is her tune

    however lovely.. loud the din
    we cannot hear her croon

ITINERANT

Dusk dripped down like drizzled mud,

    the day, now oozy, drowned beneath.

Silhouettes seemed dipped in blood

    and lay about like briared wreath.

Ebon bough and sable branch,

    titian-tinted, inky black.

Welkin's colors choosing blanch

    when wind began its rude attack.

A solitary raven flies

    as fearless 'gainst the stinging gale.

Searching under moonless skies

    for limb alight, to no avail.

LIFELINE

(paragliding)

see me fly behind the boat
    as take me for a ride, I float

CUT THE CORD and let me go
    in clouds above, on waves below

see me tethered to a friend
    when helping them replenish, mend

now it's time to GLIDE ALONE
    on rainbow sail, this bird has flown

METAPHOR

An endless stretch of traffic cones
as far as eye can see..

Driving in restricted zones
on tollways hardly free.

No, the truth is crystal clear,
am tethered to the road..

Changing lanes or changing gears,
in car and life I've slowed.

Lived for years afraid of speed,
avoiding exit ramps..

Watched for signs that bid me heed,
were ever on, my lamps.

Next time, no more GPS,
perhaps I'll ride a bike..

Or shun all wheels, will reassess
and try a bracing hike.

no in-between

(pier that looks like bridge undone)

Amidst the flattened waves
that dare not lick the
sky with crests

no rings concentric, water marking
wooden pilings' place

holding pier or path or bridge which does not
seem to span the sea, no extant
deck in view

I squint to see what could have been
if something

in-between was there, now
clearly missing, lost
or ran away...

If built and finished, risen
'bove, has left me
there alone
and flat

and like the waves
I dare not lick
the sky
my
wounds

or in-between

NUDE

painted as if carved in stone
shoulders squared and bricks for bone

still, the flesh all buff and bare
invites a gaze, our lady fair

mandolin, I hear the psalm
rising o'er a cubist's calm

not at all an angled tune
soft and flowing, curved like spoon

even as our canvas stiff
sometimes feels like petroglyph

deep inside, where songs are born
is tender, round as smooth and worn

(Pablo Picasso – "Girl with a Mandolin")

pro tem

(sitting down)

proxy for a broken heart
        the words upon a page
let me say before I start
        bestirs another age

ink to vellum, what was writ
        was never saved to cloud
no multi-tasking self be split
        nor iPhone knelling loud

feelings bled through feathered quill
        as tears on parchment dried
left my love and lost my will
        through poetry we cried

IV drips from paean's pen
        medicinal the brew
keyboard nixed is healing when
        the hieroglyphs are you

river as man

(dream big)

bountiful, his eyes fed light
to rays that slipped
between

leaves and drops of early dew
and found the spare
ravine

::

thirsty for the lumens, shed
shadow-gutted
soul

eager sipping tears with lips
as ocean bound his
goal

SHRIEK

Peculiar tale, I must admit,
a fable ETCHED in odd..

      began the day that TEXAS split
      from USA's façade.

Asleep aboard a painted train,
LOCOMOTIVE still..

      woke to news the rain in Spain
      was TEAL as mallard's quill.

        ::

The story made my RINGLETS flat,
ran screaming for the loo..

      bowl was broke, near FAUCET sat,
      and did what came to do.

I SCROUNGED about for toilet roll
when pondered how to wipe..

      the fair amount of CASSEROLE
      that felt as if unripe.

        ::

In my purse (a manly one)
where CAYENNE spices live..

POWDERED well my naked bum,
the details you'll forgive.

To CIRCUMVENT my peppered ass,
I offer this excuse..

leapt and TROUNCED with chili gas,
its fragrance keen and loose.

(photo and words prompt.. all those capitalized
were given to me to use within)

success

skimming stones will find a hole
           cut thru water, ending dash

settle neath with entry stole
           a nether home below the splash

author skipping catches break
           as arms grow weary swimming laps

time to stop and under lake
           paid to drown in words, perhaps

this morning

(apologies to reader)

    set upon my morrow chores
with words I rearrange

    mismatched sox from chest of drawers,
pen and feet feel strange

    struggled much to carve a tune,
throwing most away

    leaving moments roughly hewn,
melodies that stray

    often veering far afield
from where I thought they'd go

    odd the odes a quill can wield,
unguided goes the flow

    seems that verse is more like air
than drying ink on page

    wafting 'bout and landing there,
sweetly whispered rage

or silly things that roll your eyes,
inspire only groans

or zephyrs breezing, teasing lies,
moving rocks and stones

poetry, unruly beast,
without a whip am I

today I give you little feast,
but truly did I try

visceral

I swear, I'll but deny your claim
be rendered wholly mute

strata rooted, Christian name
an inner absolute

if and when you choose to boast
my smoking your cigar

lips and tongue from Holy Ghost
and sinking teeth too far

cocktail mixing phallic words
with pleasures that you seek

twisted omens, shaken, stirred
when served to heaven's weak

affix your fig leaf, cover well
appendages of note

or risk them singly sent to hell
on River Styx, if float

why happy..

of late I wear a wild grin
corners of my lips

    crinkle eyes and wrinkle skin
    a happiness that grips

my spirit shouts with silent smile
laughter in my teeth

    pearly whites are less my style
    than giggles rooted neath

finally advice bespoke
has reached my very soul

    give your all until you're broke
    my new and lofty goal

expect no thanks, no note of praise
as how you did your best

    joy be found in modest ways
    trite (but true) is I am blessed

Thank you

to my online mentors..

who led me to believe I might be good.

Grateful, too, for the Unsplash photographers..

who make our world infinitely

more lovely.

: :